Broken Pieces

Lakeenah Le'Shae

Cover designed by Brown Bomber Designs

Printed in the United States of America

First Printing: Aug 2020
The Scribe Tribe Publishing Group
P.O. Box 1264
Homewood, IL 60430

THE SCRIBE TRIBE
PUBLISHING GROUP

ISBN-978-1-7352568-1-8

To my beautifully and wonderfully made children, Justice and Leon. I love you more than words can ever express. Always remember, your faith must always be higher than your circumstances.

To my bonus kids, I hope you know how much you are loved and valued. This is for you too!
~Mom

Acknowledgements

Thank You, God, for choosing me for this path. You believed in me when I counted myself out.

Thank you, mom, for the unconditional love and support that you give me. You are a strong woman to be able to reuse when you were a child yourself. Thank you for keeping me.

Thank you, Mom-Mom, for always being a listening ear and for making it known that your door is always open.

Thank you Keelee, China, Shalawn, Lele, Jami and April for almost 30 years of sisterhood and for allowing me to be the person I was designed to be.

Thank you, Dr. Tyra Good, for having a consistent hand in my healing and leading me to the water.

Thank you, Aunt Lisa, for sharing those wonderful hugs with me and showing me through your words and actions that you love me.

Thank you, Pastors, for the countless conversations letting me know that God has a plan for me and to stay close to the word.

Thank you to my coworkers and those who helped and supported me in reading and the words of encouragement. I will always be grateful for you.

Thank you to those who doubted me. I was able to turn that negative into a reason to keep writing.

As I always say, if I told you I love you, I meant it with all my heart.

Love always,
Lakeenah Le'Shae

Introduction

My name is Lakeenah Le'Shae and I want to share with you why I will never give up on love. Love is what has brought me through the most difficult times and situations. The Bible says, "**Love never fails**" (1 Corinthians 13:8) and with all my heart, I feel this way. Love is what saved my life. As I write more about me and my journey, you will better understand why I embody this scripture.

Love is my language. As I look back over the years, love has always found me, even when I didn't expect it, nor was I searching for it. I love that element of surprise of it all! Love seems to be what people are afraid of these days. People say love hurts. People come and go, and people seem to not want to open up to experience what love really feels like. So, love gets pushed back further and further because people aren't willing to be open to it. This is true in familial and romantic love. Many decide that it's too much work or it's a job they aren't up for, so they push love away.

Even though love seems to always be an integral part of my life, it certainly hasn't always been easy.

This journey has taken several years for me to be able to put my words on paper, but I finally have the courage. I kept going back and forth with myself considering other people's feelings...

How will they see me after they read my book? Will they truly open their hearts to understand all that I was going through when I was "going through"? Will they try to place themselves in my shoes while turning the pages, reading my words? Will they allow themselves to cry for me, or will they judge me, be mad at me, dislike me or even verbally attack me?

For too long I chose not to write because I was concerned about how *they* may react to what I have to say. I have started and stopped writing a million times over the past 17 years because I told myself it wasn't time to tell my story but honestly, I wasn't ready to relive what I went through at such a young age. I was only 21 and things were good, but then life turned extremely bad for me. The sadness and pain I was forced to live with was crippling and so many times I felt that I couldn't go on. Every night I was inconsolable, and I'd wake up feeling mournful and broken-hearted all over again.

But God.

As I reflected on my fears, shared my concerns with a few others, and prayed to God for clarity, I realized I had already been judged, doubted, and attacked. People had already decided they didn't like me before they knew anything about me.

Why should I worry about what someone has to say about me sharing my truth?

Here is my truth:

I am a recently divorced single mother of two living in a home with about $5000 in back property taxes and a leaky roof that I cover with the blood of Jesus every time I hear it's going to rain. I am not kidding! God has found countless ways to get my attention. Now I can say I am a true woman of God and I can't understand how I lived without the faith I have now. It has been such a blessing knowing and understanding God's way. I never want to live without God for the rest of my life. I am greedy for the Lord, that's for sure. With God choosing me when He did, He was able to break me down and build me back up. Going through, I didn't know what was happening. Now on the other side, I can see that's what was going on. He had to strip me of all that wasn't for me. He took away anything that may have gotten in the way of His purpose for my life.

I must admit, I love the newly defined me. I am so much stronger now. I can understand things from a fresh perspective. No more tunnel vision. I can appreciate the small things in ways I wasn't able to in the past. I've always been able to see the good in all things but now that I have the saving grace working through me it's a much better picture. I believe that every day is an opportunity to learn so I am in this classroom of life daily, willing to learn. Not a day goes by that I don't take something from it. I learn from some of the closest people to me but also from strangers. I'm learning to be a better me, a better mom, a better daughter, and a better woman of God.

Recently, I reconnected with my very first love, Mitch. We've always held a special place in each other's hearts; Mitch has always been a true friend and reminded me of my worth. We met when we were teenagers and went our separate ways, but we always seem to cross paths just when one of us needs a lifeline. It's like a reality check for us both. We make a point to let each other know how important we are to one another and remind each other that our dreams can come true if we believe and keep pushing. Mitch has encouraged me and pushed me so much. He was one of the people who suggested I tell my whole truth. To hear this man speak about what he sees in me is breathtaking. Any man can talk about what they see as far as a walk, the way someone talks, or how they dress or smell. Not Mitch. He has said some of the most profound things to me that had me wondering how this man loves me like this. I've never experienced anyone seeing me the way his eyes see me. I always have to take a moment to process what he says. I once had to share one of his profound messages with a coworker. She read it and her response was, "Wow, Tink. I have never had anyone express themselves like that about me. He really thinks the world of you." She then asked how long I had known him. My response was two decades. One of the things he said to me in one of our deep calls was that he wanted us to share our fears. Now that may not sound too deep to you, but to me that spoke volumes. Do you know anyone who really *wants* to put themselves on a platter to be served up for possible judgment or be put in a vulnerable place? This is far from common in any relationship. But because of the level of trust he has for me, he was willing.

I am forever grateful for him being one of my biggest fans and helping me feel like I'm the greatest ever made. He is part of the reason that you get to read these words.

So, let's do this! Turn the page and enter my world, my truth – the good, the bad, and everything in between.

Part One

A BEAUTIFUL NIGHTMARE

Chapter One

It was just my mom and me for much of my life. We moved to the north side of Pittsburgh, Pennsylvania 2 I was a freshman in high school. We lived in an income-based housing project called Spring Hill Apartments; they were fairly new and still quiet and laid back.

Moving to the north side was a challenging experience because I never felt welcomed. Gang violence was just beginning to ramp up in Pittsburgh and I resided on the east side in the neighborhood we called Lincoln, ever since we relocated from York, PA to get a "fresh start" when I was in middle school. Even though Pittsburgh is not a huge city, most neighborhoods just didn't mix well, and I was the new girl once again, with no friends. But after a while, I had a few good homies in Spring Hill. Unlike many of my new friends, I didn't attend one of the neighborhood schools. I went to a vocational school on the south side, but I would meet my new neighborhood friends at the mailboxes after we all finished our homework. Everyone would bring snacks and come over to my house to chill into the evening.

When I was about 17, I got my second job at a popular neighborhood corner store. It was just your typical 'hood store. Folks would come in for their penny candy, fresh baked cookies, bread, cigarettes, toilet paper, lottery, and even good conversation most days. There were so many people in and out of the store all the time. Young and old, babies, all walks of life. Folks would even come in to sell their stolen goods. There were plenty of days that I needed a payday advance to purchase film, lotions, and other things that they were selling. I met so many people daily including the older man with the handicap arm who always wanted single cigarettes and the man that would sniff the glue and dance for some treats. The little kids who came in smiled at my jokes and graciously thanked me for offering up what they were short for chips or bags of Swedish fish bagged up in counts of twenty-five.

Then there were the guys who came in the store who would try to holler at me, but I paid them no mind. Most gave up trying after a while but there was one who would not stop. He was the one who caught my eye. I think it was his sense of humor that I was drawn to.

David was a piece of work.

His sense of humor was unmatched. Whenever he stopped in the store, it was guaranteed that he would have me cracking up. He smelled so good, dressed nice and his glasses were sharp. He was so handsome with his glasses on. I rarely dared to say anything to David during those early encounters at the store, but he always seemed to have something to say to me. Some days he would actually leave me speechless. And that's pretty hard to do. Sometimes I would think to myself, *how did he come up with that?* I was still young and inexperienced with guys, so I certainly didn't think I was mature enough for a guy who was forever saying all the right stuff.

While his whole crew stayed fly and dressed to the nines, none compared to David in my eyes. One of the things that impressed me about David was that he didn't partake in the normal stunts for my attention. He didn't lurk around the store waiting to see how far our conversation may go that day, nor did he ever try to take anything off the shelf without paying to see if I thought it was cool. David was different.

One day, out of the blue, he brought me lunch during my shift. He walked in and looked at me as if he were looking through me. He said, "Here, I picked you up something to eat." My face indicated that I was puzzled but I was appreciative because I love to eat. From that day forward, anytime he saw me at the store he brought me something to eat; that allowed me to see him almost every time I was at work. He never asked if I wanted food before he purchased it. I was amazed that he wasn't concerned about possibly wasting money if I didn't want it. His kind gesture was to simply ensure that I was okay. It's not that he thought that I needed food or anything. Even though my frame is small, and it may have appeared that I needed a few meals, I'm sure he was just being nice. He knew that I didn't make much money and I couldn't leave the store to get anything to eat.

After plenty of times in and out of the store, David was no longer a stranger or someone that I was afraid would harm me. As time progressed, he continued to express an interest in me. David was intentional in his efforts to let me know that he wanted me and that he was going to have me. I would just smile, and think, *okay, David!*

One night I went to Sweet Georgia Browns, a neighborhood bar, with a coworker from the store who was also a DJ. I wasn't old enough to get in but because I got there early with the DJ, I was good. Since I wasn't a drinker *and* I was underage, I chose a slow gin and orange juice as my drink of the night. Honestly, I had no idea what the difference between a slow gin and any other type of gin was but my barely-older than me cousin, Likah, had taken me out partying with her one night and that was the drink she ordered. It wasn't too strong, but it was good and pretty so it stuck with me. Besides, that drink made me look like an adult in a bar setting instead of looking like a kid with no business being there.

My slow gin and OJ may have worked to make me look like I belonged, but it did nothing for my feelings. I felt out of place for obvious reasons, but as I watched everything that walked in and out of the bar for hours, I became increasingly uncomfortable. Bored, I just sat there and pretended to love my drink.

Then I saw David walk in!

I was wide open and excited to greet him. He was with several of his cousins and I was still close enough for my DJ friend to keep an eye out, but it was as though we were the only two in the bar at that point. I was happy to see a familiar face, but also nervous because I wasn't at work and felt vulnerable in such an open, adult space. Our conversation that night would lead to many more nights together. However, that night I went home, as I should have.

♡

After that first night, things moved quickly, and I couldn't remember what life was like before him. We had an instant connection; it felt like we had been with each other forever.

We got together often.

I didn't have a car and my mom was usually at work so David would pick me up from work every night and make sure I got into the house safely. We went out to dinner a few times a week and sometimes we would just ride around and talk or enjoy each other's company before he dropped me off. If we were away from each other, it wasn't for exceptionally long periods. Like *30-Day Fiancé*, we were an item almost instantly. It was such a nice feeling to be in the arms of a man that loved me.

My own man.

At 18, I felt I was doing well for my age. I had just started my first semester at the local community college, I still had my corner store job which allowed me to set my hours so as not to interfere with my life, and I'd already met the man I wanted to spend my life with. A whole man who wanted to love on me and who wanted to make me his everything. My thoughts weren't at all focused on my studies and I didn't have any greater desire than having a family of my own. *Do I stay in school or do I stop wasting my time?* Since I had a wonderful man that was ready to give me just what I wanted, it didn't take me long to make a decision; I withdrew from school immediately and David and I started rocking even harder.

One day as David and I were driving around talking, he told me that he no longer wanted me to work at the store. There was always a lot of traffic in and out of the store, some good and some bad. But since I was David's girl and that was his 'hood, I understood that it just wasn't a good look. I had been working since I was 14 so that demand, heavily cloaked by David's concern for my safety, came as a pretty big surprise to me. All he desired to do was take care of me and spend time together. He promised that we would find a better position for me within a few months. That was when I knew that David genuinely cared for me and our future together.

David began to introduce me to his kids, family, and friends. When we met, David already had six kids. He had his first when he was just a couple months shy of 16. He told me that he wanted to have a *real* family of his own; he wanted a lot of kids and for them to all live under the same roof. David wanted to give his kids what we both lacked growing up. He was such a great, caring, and nurturing father. I was so in love with seeing David be a dad, taking care of the kids, and making time for them daily. I am inclined to believe it was because I had never experienced a hands-on father in my own home, nor had many of my friends or family members. Growing up, I did not witness too many dads who stepped up and took on day-in and day-out responsibility for their children. It was more common to see the mothers grinding, sacrificing, and working hard for better lives for their kids.

My mom was rarely in town during those days. She was dating a man who lived in Cleveland, so my occasional overnight stays with David effortlessly turned into multiple nights, then weeks and next thing I knew we lived together. I didn't require much but what I didn't bring with me David made sure he supplied. He wanted me to be comfortable. He showered me with gifts, more than I could ever ask for. I was living every woman's dream as David loved to shop for me and the kids. I never had to go to the mall for anything. He enjoyed seeing the surprised looks on our faces each time any of us opened a bag from one of our favorite stores. He knew all our sizes, so there was never a need to make any return trips. David knew just what we liked, and he knew what he liked as well so there was always a special bag from Victoria's Secret waiting for me in our bedroom. David knew how to make us feel special.

As I said, he was different.

About six months later, I started working for one of the city's largest hospitals as a unit clerk. That job offered me the possibility of employment stability. There was opportunity for growth within the company and that was a huge upgrade from the corner store. I was enjoying my new grown-up job. I wasn't the breadwinner and David didn't expect me to make a bunch of money, or even spend the little that I did make. He was perfectly fine with just being with me. He was in love with me and not what I had on paper. I wish there were more people in the world like him. David recognized my value, but my job gave me a purpose and allowed me to bring something other than my love to the table.

The job was a good fit for my family, and I felt extremely proud that I was able to provide medical insurance for David. As a diabetic, he desperately needed that because his medicine was not cheap. With my insurance, David was able to get his medicine without having to pay exorbitant out-of-pocket costs.

David did not hold back when it came to expressing his aspirations for the future. He always told me how he felt, and we would dream out loud together. We talked about moving out of town or starting our family business so we could come and go as we pleased. David's other plans included having ten more kids. I was willing to commit to three babies, but ten was out of the question!

♡

My mom was getting married and starting her new life with her husband and I was starting my life as a young adult with a few kids that would soon call me their bonus mom. My mom was relocating to Ohio, but I was left in good hands with Mr. David Taron Williams. He started calling me his wife without hesitation. In conversation he said, "my wife." Even his cousins would reference me as his wife. Of course,

David would laugh but he knew that I was an integral part of his future from the beginning.

We weren't together a year before he bought me an engagement ring.

I remember that day as if it were yesterday. It wasn't anything big and extravagant, but it was perfect for us. We were at Monroeville Mall shopping and we walked into the jewelry store to browse. He spotted a ring and asked me if I liked it and I said yes. I did not expect him to ask me anything about the ring, so when he asked me if I wanted it, I was a bit taken aback. As I looked him in his eyes, I responded, "If you want me to have it then yes, I want it."

He put a deposit down and told me to go home, get the rest of the money, and return to pick my ring up. I did just that. I went back that same day and got my ring! I was ecstatic to go back and pick up the ring that I didn't expect, nor did I have to pressure him to get. I was happy to pick up the ring that was far off my radar but not far off his. He didn't get down on bended knee, but he did make sure I knew it was a promise that he would marry me. He made sure I knew I was the love of his life and he wanted to marry me as soon as we were able. We were in full-blown love. I felt it in his words and in his touch. If this man didn't love me then I didn't know what love was.

♡

We traveled a lot.

Our first trip abroad was to the Bahamas. It was the first time that I flew on an airplane. I was thrilled as I reflected on my life. A girl who had only been on road trips to family functions was on a plane taking exotic vacations. David never made me feel like I deserved anything less. He took care of me in ways that I couldn't dream about. I loved talking to David and being in his presence and our long flight to the Bahamas was no exception. He opened up to me and revealed a side of him that I had never seen before. He showed a vulnerability that made me fall in love with him more and more. It wasn't just the altitude of the plane that made me feel like I was on cloud nine!

After we arrived in paradise, he continued our fairytale adventure by showering me with many gifts. It was hard to accept those high-priced items because I had such strong women in my life encouraging me to be independent. But he also drew out a vulnerability in me. It was a whirlwind of emotions that I never wanted to end. I realized that's what I wanted--someone who wanted me to dream big. Someone who encouraged me to reach for the stars. Someone who put me on a pedestal. And he did all of that! He was the one that I wanted to take care of me, and I wanted to take care of him. I was in heaven sitting on the beach with the man I loved and gazing at the stars that we would reach together.

Then there was Miami. I was never a materialistic person, but this man wanted me to have the best! We were celebrating our anniversary and he wanted to shower me with more gifts. I wouldn't allow him to spoil me with gifts that time though. That wasn't why we were there. It wasn't necessary to spend thousands of dollars just because we were on vacation or celebrating our anniversary. He appreciated me for being the kind of woman that didn't care about the latest designs or keeping up with Joneses. But my David really wanted to tear the mall up and rightfully so! That mall in Miami was like an adult candy store. It had only the best designer shops. The merchandise sold there was so grand that some of the stores had armed guards standing outside the doors. The Louis Vuitton store lured us in, but we were able to control ourselves. We left Miami with a few things.

David was one of my first teachers as an adult. He taught me so much about life from my personal affairs to business matters. He showed me that it's okay to laugh and have a good time. He also taught me to know when it was time to shut it down and say what you mean and mean what you say. David helped to develop me into the kind of mother that I wanted to be.

I loved it when he taught me how to cook new things. Now, I come from a long line of family that can cook. My mom and Mom-Mom (my grandmother) are wonderful cooks. But when my man began to show me things, I was eager to learn. It was different learning from him because of the intimacy shared between the two of us. I was young and ready to cook for my family. He showed me how to make a few of his favorites: fried green tomatoes, oxtails, and rice in the pressure cooker. I was cooking my butt off! I learned to cook all meals, but breakfast was my shot. Everyone knows that breakfast is the most important meal of the day, so I had to get it right. Sausage and eggs were especially important. David showed me how to do it the right way. He made sausage links, but he would first boil them in water for a few minutes and then turn the heat down on low and cut the casing off. Once the casing was off, he would finish cooking the sausage in butter until golden brown.

Thanks to David, I am now a stickler about how my eggs are prepared. We only ate our eggs scrambled hard and they must be cooked with all windows and doors closed. Don't ask me why but that was one of David's pet peeves that I adopted. I did not understand at first, but now I will not eat eggs if I know that they were cooked with a door or window open. My family and friends think I am crazy, but they have learned to adjust to my request. If you think I am crazy, try it for yourself and see what smell you get when that fresh air hits your eggs. Just make sure I am not there! You will thank David and me later.

♡

David was a hustler, but he also worked a traditional job. He was a man of the streets, but not one of those guys you would see in those Scarface or Mafia movies. He wasn't going to look at you with a death stare or cut your finger off if you spoke out of turn, but he wasn't to be played with either. David wanted everyone to be good. He would help whoever he could, within reason. Sometimes he would do too much and realize his error afterward. His heart was big, and he always just wanted to be a provider for his family.

We enjoyed each other and had goals for one another. We had conversations with our friend Bobby and his wife about owning our businesses where we would all be involved so we wouldn't have to punch a clock anymore. David and Bobby didn't want us to have to work anymore. We enjoyed being with Bobby and his family. When we met them, it was like we were starting our little circle from scratch. It was like we were all family. I was ready for a whole adult life with this David. Bobby would always laugh because I only called David by his real name. I wasn't calling him any of his nicknames unless I was being funny. I for sure wasn't calling him Dave or Lush. What I look like saying, "Hey, Lush." I was his woman, not his homeboy.

We balanced one another out. I was able to be there for him after a long day of work and be his release from whatever he may have gone through during the day. I was able to have his kids home at night so he could see them before they went to bed and see them off to school in the morning. I was able to give him a sense of peace and he was my rock. David was able to make me feel like everything was going to be alright. He constantly reminded me that I was his number one regardless of what I thought about myself.

I remember one of my first interactions with one of the kid's moms. She called to speak to David and between the time I answered the phone and before he came to get the phone from me, the mom had a few choice words to say about me to whoever was with her. I heard it all! Now what she was saying wasn't important to me, but I told David every word and he checked her on the spot. That situation was foreign to me because I never had confrontations with anyone. He checked her to the point that she called me back some days later and apologized for what she said. It's not that I didn't expect him to stand up for me, but I was overjoyed that he consistently showed me that he wanted everyone to know he chose me. David made it crystal clear that everyone needed to respect me!

He was my rock and we were solid.

Some of my favorite memories with the kids were when they were attending primary school; there were so many events that we would attend. One of the most memorable was when I made cupcakes for the girls' 100th day of school. I was so proud to be their bonus mom. I made so many cupcakes to take to school between the two of them. Now, I'm not saying I made 100 cupcakes, but I knew I made a lot of cupcakes and remember writing the number 100 on top of them. Score for the bonus mom! The teachers loved my idea. Oh, and that was all my creativity because Pinterest wasn't even out then. I took my job as a bonus mom very seriously because I was in training to be a mom of my own one day. We would have sleepovers with as many kids as possible because as I said, David wanted that feeling of all his kids under one roof. They would have ripping sessions and movie nights. There were so many of us that family outings required us to get a van. We had multiple cars and trucks, but I preferred to have the entire family in one vehicle. He spoiled me with so much love that I wanted to be with him as much as possible.

All of David's immediate family were amazing to me. They treated me very well. One year for Mother's Day, his sister Joy planned a brunch or dinner. I didn't think anything of it. I was young with no children that I had actually birthed, so I didn't expect to be a part of the Mother's Day festivities. My new big sister, Joy, invited me to a five-star restaurant with an amazing view and some of her closest friends. She told me that I was a mother and deserved to be there. That was such a wonderful feeling. I felt so loved, wanted, and appreciated by her and her friends. Joy loved David and me so much that she asked us to be her son's godparents. We were honored and I was shocked. Joy not only chose her brother, but she selected me as well. She could have easily just chosen him and one of her friends for that responsibility. But no. It was both of us that she wanted. I gained a sister that absolutely loved me because of my union with an incredible man named David.

♡

Not long after our engagement, we became pregnant with our first child. Our dreams were starting to manifest!

David bought us a house that was a fixer upper. I mean the house needed to be gutted. It was pretty much a shell. No floors or cabinets in the kitchen. No railings going up to the second floor. It was a total renovation. During the renovation, we continued to stay in the house we were renting. There was no way that we could stay in our new home while sparks were flying, and wood dust covered the place. Contractors were installing everything that you can think of. The conditions were not suitable for a pregnant woman, or anyone for that matter.

David wanted the house to be completed before the baby's due date in January, which meant David wanted it to be done by Thanksgiving so we could get settled in before our bundle of joy arrived. He was hopeful that we could even host some of our family for the holiday season. During our two sonogram visits, our baby would not allow us to see whether we were expecting a prince or a princess. It was exciting to experience the mystery of not knowing the gender; I was just delighted to know that we were in it together. Of course, we were still anxious to know what we were having, but I'm unsure if David wanted to know just so he was informed and prepared or if he needed another reason to shop!

Countless days and nights were spent at the new house as the contractors were getting it ready. David was so wonderful about including me in all the details of the renovation operation. Even though I fully trusted him all his ideas, he wanted to share those moments with his soon-to-be wife. The only thing I wanted was a big kitchen that could accommodate all of us while we cooked meals for our family. I also desired a big tub so I could take a bath every opportunity I got. Oh, and I requested that the tub was big enough for us both to bathe together. I was not willing to compromise on those two desires. Those were reasonable requests for him to fulfill; David would never have said no to quality time and meals with his family or a bath with the love of his life.

By the third trimester, I couldn't contribute much at the house, but I accompanied David on plenty of runs to the hardware store and Construction Junction. Man, that place is amazing! I was surprised at how many nice things we found in Construction Junction. We were able to find enough railings for our first and second floors. I couldn't believe how they were a complete match to the cherry wood that was already on the steps. Our kitchen was beautiful. Everything in that room was brand new. We had cream cabinets with marble floors that matched the cabinets perfectly. The stainless-steel appliances that filled the kitchen were the icing on the cake.

Our home originally had six bedrooms, but we knocked down a wall to enlarge our master bedroom. Our kids' rooms were on the third floor and fostered a sense of family with a Jack and Jill layout. The guest and baby rooms shared the floor with our master suite. David designed his room or what I called our family room in the basement. He nicknamed it the Boom Boom Room. It was laid out! We had classic, standup video games which included: Ms. Pac Man, Donkey Kong, and Centipede. They were the highlight of the basement. There was a fully functional bar with lights that would give a nice glow at night while watching a movie. David ensured that there was an extra bathroom complete with a shower in the basement so guests would not have to utilize our bedroom for any reason. The Boom Boom Room was such a comfortable space where David and the kids spent a lot of time together.

We turned that house into a home!

The staircase was so nice and wide that we wanted to get married in our house. I envisioned myself walking down the steps with my beautiful gown as I gazed at my man.

Our family functions were off the hook! My mom and stepdad came down from Ohio to kick it with us. Our local family would always be there. His cousins and my family got together even when David and I were not present. There were no such things as my friends and his friends. We were all friends and family. We didn't believe in separating anything. Our blended family was beautiful, and I loved all his kids. They learned to call me mom without force. It was a natural thing that they decided, and I loved every bit of it.

The oldest girls' mother was so sweet to me. I never had any issues with her. Even today, if we see each other, it is nothing but love. There was once a chickenhead that was in pursuit of my man. Coincidentally, the girls' mom worked with the girl and was ready to give a good whooping. She knew that I wasn't one for drama or anything negativity. She was willing to go to bat for me. Not for David, but for me. That chickenhead would have never seen that butt whooping coming, but I never signed off on it. She just wasn't worth it. However, it was a great feeling to know that the girls' mom cared enough for me to try to battle for me if needed. I never got to know the other children's mothers, but the girls' mom and I will forever be cool.

David wanted more kids with me. He said I handled pregnancy well and I agreed with him. I didn't really have any aches or pains during my nine months and one day of carrying our baby. Overall, I functioned well while I was pregnant. I enjoyed everything from feeling all the kicks to the uncomfortable nights. I felt like pregnancy was my thing; I had mastered how to carry a baby. My confidence levels shot through the roof as I thought, '*I could do this a few more times if I wanted to.*'

Now, I did hurt enough to get my back rubbed. I wasn't missing out on his touch on my body. David was as much a touchy-feely person as I was. If I moved wrong or looked like I was hurting in any way in his presence, he was on it. I ate up all that attention. I loved that man so much for loving me. I wasn't big enough to wear maternity clothes so he wasn't able to buy those kinds of things for me as we wanted, but we were able to buy a size or two bigger in shirts only; my pants size didn't go up at all. The older kids seemed to be ecstatic that they had a new sibling on the way. We were all excited that our blended family was growing with love.

Everything was perfect and we were patiently awaiting the arrival of our bundle of joy.

♡

Of course, David wasn't perfect, but he was a good guy. *They say you must take the good with the bad, right?!*

One day, I was out visiting some of my friends I hadn't seen since I left the north side. I was minding my own business, basking in my pregnant glow, shopping, and I overheard the conversation of two other women. There I was, head over heels happy, soon-to-be-married with the new house, new family and a baby on the way. I was in my glory! Then, I heard one of the women say her name.

I said, "Oh you're Lisa?"

Sarcastically, she responded, "Yeah, and!?"

Her tone left me thinking, *'what the hell?!'*

But I disregarded her initial response thinking that she may have had the wrong idea. Despite of her tone, I happily shared that I was quite sure that she was my fiancé's manicurist, and then I stood there smiling and waiting for her to change her tune.

    Why did I say that?!

She began a rant that left me speechless...

"Did he tell you he was my man? Do you want to step outside?"

I had no words! I was utterly confused.

At that point, I was completely crushed because I was innocent in the situation. I had no clue what she was talking about and I didn't know what to do. Immediately, I phoned David to tell him what happened and let him know that he needed to handle it. I was still at a loss for words and not sure what to do or say next. I just knew that I wasn't going to fight her about *my* man, and I wasn't jeopardizing our baby because of her accusations.

David knew that he was in hot grease. There was no way to ignore me or the situation that he had created. By the time I got home, he had already had a plan to rectify the circumstances. Yes, he was wrong for dealing with that woman, especially since we headed for marriage. But David assured me that he would take care of that chick and that I would never have to worry about her again. Naturally, I got a little jazzy to remind him that I was serious about him handling it. My instructions were all directed towards David because I was never worried about her in the first place. Honestly, I don't know if he ever saw that woman again or if he checked her like he did his kids' mom, but I never experienced any more issues going forward. Besides, it was almost time for us to welcome our baby. I was way too excited about our growing family to be consumed with nonsense!

♡

Our baby was due on January 18, 2002 but when the big day rolled around, I felt no pain or cramping. Hours had passed and I started missing my man because he was not home. He was out kicking it with his cousin, Terry. My initial thought was that he was probably out pre-gaming the celebration of our child's birth. So, Dana, who was Terry's girlfriend at the time, and I got on the phone and devised a plan to get our guys home. We knew they were together. Our genius plan was to tell them that I was in labor. *Yes, that's it! Let's tell them I'm in some pain*. We did just that. The guys told Dana to drive me to the hospital and they would meet us there.

Wouldn't you know that on our way to the hospital I actually went into labor!

Just after midnight, sudden pains started to erupt all through my stomach and back. On top of that excruciating pain, I was starving! The Dirty O was right down the street and the hungry, pregnant woman was forbidden from eating anything. The Dirty O was the spot to visit when you needed a fix of greasy fries, hot dogs, cheap pizza, and the like. That night, I would have given anything for a beef hot dog and greasy fries. Instead, Dana gave me a red Jolly Rancher as a quick, temporary fix. Desperate for anything, I ate it, and just as fast as I swallowed that candy, I spit it up. I guess my baby said, "Heck no! I don't want that candy. I'm ready to meet my mommy and daddy!" Thank God that David and his cousin arrived at the hospital shortly after we did. I was ready for his hands to rub on my back and stomach. His voice was so calming to my pains. Truthfully, I don't know if it was David's voice and touch that was soothing me or if it was the legal drugs kicking in or if it was because we were truly in love. I think it was probably a combination of all those things.

The delivery was very smooth. I wasn't in labor long at all.

I don't have the answers to those questions that *they* ask new moms.
"Do I remember how many hours you were in labor? Do you know how many inches she was?" No! But I do recall that it was a quick delivery and my baby was healthy.

I was just happy and ready to eat. That grilled cheese was so good. It was like the best thing since sliced bread.

Welcome to the world, sweet girl of ours.

When I held Baby Justice in my arms, I couldn't believe that I'd just had a baby! My man and I had just pushed out a baby together. A baby that looked like her father with my eyes. David didn't miss a beat. Even though he was nervous, he was the best coach. He was strong for me. Even now, I can visualize us at the hospital. Mr. Jokester wanted to keep his blue scrub bonnet on so everyone would know that he was the proud father of a new baby!

Finally, we could go purchase pink and purple clothes since little Miss Missy wanted to keep her legs closed. I prayed that she kept that closed leg energy! At our baby shower we received outfits, but they were unisex colors. You know, the greens and yellows and whites. So, everyone wanted to wait until the baby was born to buy gender-appropriate clothes. Our friends Bobby and his wife came to the hospital with the biggest gift box ever. It was wrapped so nicely and full of purple things. Everything that you can think of was in that box. They really splurged on the baby girl. David and I were so happy that we had something else to call our own. He was already mentally preparing for more pregnancies with me.

Jus had her own room, but she slept with us. The only time she saw her room was when I wanted to walk around the second floor to rock her to sleep or when we visited her room to look at her tons of clothes. We were so blessed to have family and friends that loved us. I remember Joy came over to the house to see the baby and she brought the cutest thing. She gave Justice some pink Gucci baby booties. Joy, Joy, Joy!

Justice was a good sleeper for a newborn baby. I am one that loves to get my rest, so she was a perfect match for me. The perfect baby. I tried to do the breastfeeding thing for our baby, but I just couldn't do it. On one hand, I wanted to do it, but I also didn't think it was fair that I had to be the only one getting up in the middle of the night for feedings. Pretty selfish right? Wrong! I wanted and needed to sleep, and daddy and Justice bonded during those 2 am feeding times. So, I breastfed Justice for 2.2 seconds and they were able to have their daddy-daughter time quite often.

Before long, it was time for me to go back to work. As much as I wanted to stay home with my kids, I had to return. However, I was blessed with peace of mind as I returned to work because Justice was in trusted care. My Mom-Mom, Britney, and Ms. Penny provided her with excellent care. I trusted each one of them with my baby girl. Of course, I had known my Mom-Mom all my life because that's my grandmother. Britney is my younger cousin but because Mom-Mom raised her, she was more like my baby sister. Ms. Penny had her own daycare, but she is also my little cousin's grandmother so she's basically family. She was able to keep Justice so we could return to work with no worries. David and I both loved Ms. Penny very much and she loved seeing us together. She always complimented us on the love she saw between the two of us. She always told me that I had a good one. Whenever David picked Justice up, Ms. Penny enjoyed her conversation with him. She said he always had such nice things to say about me and that his face lit up when he mentioned my name. Every girl wants to know that her man exudes the type of love that she is feeling on the inside. I knew that I had a good guy. We were a great team.

Things seemed to be perfect.

We were both working jobs we enjoyed. David was a concrete tester for a local company outside of the city. He really enjoyed working on projects in the city and being in the lab to see the other side of it. We had everything we needed and a lot of what we wanted. We were so in love with each other, with our children and with our new home.

Chapter Two

We had little time to enjoy our new home, baby, and kids together before things shifted. In what seemed like an instant, life was forever changed.

On April 29, 2003, David took me to my favorite salad place, Mitchell's Restaurant, for lunch. They had the best house ranch dressing. Since the hospital was so close, it was nothing for David to pick me up for lunch. I got my food and David and I sat in the truck, ate and talked about our future with our family. He told me that he was ready to leave Pittsburgh and be done with the life that we had here. Our plan was to move to Atlanta and be married by the end of the summer.

I returned to work knowing that I would see him at home later that evening when we planned to go to a boxing match in Monroeville. We went to the boxing match and picked up our daughter, Justice, from Mom-Mom's house. We went home and did our normal night routine. He turned on the house alarm as was customary. We always put it on 'away' mode as if we weren't home. We could walk around upstairs but we couldn't go downstairs without the alarm going off. That was fine because we had all we needed for the night. Snacks, baby bottles and something to drink just in case his "suga got low," as he would say. David constantly used his diabetes as a tactic to get his way. That excuse let him eat first at family functions and had me doing the things that he did not feel like doing but knew that I would take care of without question. That man was crazy and crazy about me. I loved every bit of it. My family and I went to bed for the night. Justice was asleep right beside us because she always slept with us.

I was stirred awake when I heard something, but I wasn't sure what it was I heard. I don't know if David heard anything when I did but once we both heard it, we realized that we needed to wake up fast. Unfortunately, we didn't realize what was happening quickly enough.

"Wake the f*%& up! Get up now!"

There were four men, dressed in all black in our bedroom forcing us to get up by gunpoint. There was no time to reach for the gun we purchased a few weeks prior; we were new homeowners and we wanted protection to be able to defend what was ours. I didn't believe we would ever need it.

I was wrong.

> *Who are these men and why are they here? What do they want with us?*

Our security alarm never sounded, nor did it alarm the police. No calls to our cell or house phones from the alarm company. No alarming noises to make intruders want to leave.

Before I knew it, they pulled us out of bed and shook us up a bunch and threatened to kill us if we didn't give them what they wanted. I didn't have anything on but my red Victoria's Secret cotton underwear. My whole body was exposed for some strange men to see. They saw my vulnerability, my insecurities, and my love for my family. I was in a state of panic, as I tried to gather my thoughts. I cried and wondered how that was happening to us.

Why would someone want to do anything like this to us?

I had to grab Justice and hold her tightly so she wouldn't be afraid. I tried to cover Justice and in a special way, Justice covered me. She didn't even cry, but I cried hysterically as I tried to think of how we could get out of the situation.

David tried so hard to make them understand that we didn't have anything. They weren't trying to hear anything that he said. They didn't allow me to get anything to put on. They told me that I wasn't anything to look at.

David, Justice, and I were forced to the first floor by the intruders. I'm not sure what David said to the guys but whatever he said led us downstairs into the kitchen and out the back door. We could see that was the way they came into our home. They were forcing us out the back door into our family van. At some point, one of the guys left from where we all were to go to some unknown place. Before exiting the house, I asked them if I could get David's insulin since he was diabetic. They allowed me to get it out of the refrigerator. I wasn't really thinking but he needed food after his insulin. So, that was pointless to be concerned about it. Even though he wasn't going to be thinking about food while being kidnapped. They allowed David to put pants and a button-up shirt on. They only allowed me to put David's navy blue, thick, cotton robe on and my stepdaughter's black Reeboks. We went out the back door and I saw why the one guy disappeared. He pulled the van into the yard and closed the gate. We were forced into the van and one of the guys got out of the van to open the gate so we could drive out. Before he approached the gate, he took off his mask. I guessed so he wouldn't alarm anyone walking or driving past. Once he opened the gate, he didn't think to pull his mask back down. I was able to see his face clear as day. I had never seen him a day in my life.

Who is this guy?! Who are these people?!

Just before he got back in the van, he pulled it back down.

David's shirt was not buttoned up and I was half-naked. We drove up Robinson Boulevard and down to Allegheny River Boulevard. At some point between Allegheny River Boulevard and Saltsburg Road, one of the four guys got out the van. I don't recall any conversation about why he got out or what his next move would be. I don't think that they thoroughly planned out their home invasion. They probably thought it would be an in and out thing. Go in and get what they wanted and go on with their lives. But it didn't quite go that way. Instead, it was three guys and the three of us.

At that point, I had no clue where we were headed. I sat quietly as I contemplated a way to save my baby girl and my future husband. My heart was so heavy with countless emotions. I knew that I wasn't ready to die but if I had to go, I was leaving with my family. It's so crazy that I don't remember saying one prayer the whole time. The life that I live now, I pray throughout the day, every day. But I know that God was with us the whole time. He wasn't ready for me to go yet. Now, being the spiritual woman that I am, I don't go a day without talking to my Father. So, I know that He has been with me and chose me before I chose Him.

David made a call to an unknown person. We ended up at some apartments in Spring Hill. A female came out with a bag. I didn't know why we went to her house and I for sure didn't understand how she could possibly help us out of the situation. But whatever was in that bag wasn't what they wanted. Or at least it wasn't enough. To this day, I still don't know what was in that bag, but they were unhappy with the contents. They showed a lot of anger and exchanged a lot of words that indicated their dissatisfaction. I began to beg and plead with them to let us go and that we wouldn't tell anyone about the kidnapping. I told them that we would leave town first thing in the morning if they would let us go. After I said that, the one mean-looking kidnapper responded, "We ain't no petty thieves."

I was angry, afraid, and confused.

> How can someone that broke into someone's home be choosy about what they want? How is that even possible?

We drove off and headed down Route 28. The driver made a detour and pulled over so they could discuss their next move. It was clear they weren't prepared for all the extra mishaps that transpired. We pulled over down in the Etna area and David and I had words with the guys and with each other.

The kidnappers expressed how pissed off they were. It was as if they were almost certain that they were going to get something from us at the house, but they didn't. They continued to discuss the next steps in their plan. Meanwhile, David begged them to let us go...

BOOM!

I was in complete shock.

One of the men shot David in his leg!

"NOOOOOOO!" I screamed.

David and I were sitting side by side. The feeling that I felt through my body when that shot was fired to his leg, felt as if I was also shot. I don't know if it was because we were pretty much touching or if it was because of the extreme connection we shared with one another.

I felt helpless!

   Lord, what am I to do?

He was in so much pain! *We* were in so much pain. It was at that moment when I lost all hope that we would make it out of that van alive.

What if we can't get them what they want? Will they shoot me next?

I couldn't believe our baby girl was a part of that horrifying experience. It broke my heart that I was unable to protect her, and I could see it on David's face how much it pained him not to be able to protect us from the evil that had found us.

I felt like I was in a nightmare I would never wake up from.

The kidnappers were still trying to figure things out and I continued to plead with them as I looked down and saw the gun between one of the guy's legs. Because my hands weren't tied, I was able to reach for the gun. I attempted to formulate a plan to save my family and possibly harm the other guys, but the thoughts going through my head didn't make any sense to me. Everything seemed like it would have ended with us all hurt, if not dead.

Who do I shoot first? What if the gun doesn't go off when I go to pull the trigger? What if they try to do something to my baby to show us that they aren't playing any more games with us?

I'd never shot a gun before, so I had no idea how it would end. I decided to continue to hold my baby and hope for everything to be over soon. Silently, I hoped that someone or something would come to our rescue.

BAM!

I was hit in the head with a gun.

It was the gun that we purchased to protect us.

I was in pain, but the shock was so intense that I barely remember feeling the physical pain. My concern lied with David and Justice. I forced my own feelings aside.

David was losing a ton of blood and I thought if we did make it out alive, my baby was going to be scarred for life. Justice did not cry at all. She was very calm and just sat there. I know that old idiom says that God takes care of the babies. He had to be comforting her.

At some point, I realized the van was moving again. I had no idea where we were headed, but we had just reached the Highland Park Bridge.

David told me to call my uncle.

"Yeah, call your uncle," one of the kidnappers taunted.

I have so many uncles, but I knew exactly which one he was talking about because they had become closer than the others.

When David handed me his cell phone, I was shocked!

How did he manage to get it out of the house?

"What am I supposed to say?" I asked as I dialed frantically.

"Say you need '*life insurance*,'" David quickly responded.

It was at that precise moment that I knew that the abduction had taken another turn for the worse. I tried my best to remain calm, so my uncle knew how serious my words were.

"I need $150,000 in life insurance," I blurted out as he picked up the phone.

"What are you talking about, Tink? What's going on?"

I just repeated what I was told to say over and over again. Soon he understood exactly what I said.

"Tell them *to do what they have to do*," he snarked and then hung up on me.

> *Did he really just hang up on me? How am I supposed to tell the man I love that my uncle has turned his back on me...on us...his family?!*

Hesitantly, I repeated what my uncle said.

"He said, 'tell them to do what they have to do.'"

I felt like we had just been handed a death sentence by the guys who entered our family home with the assistance of my own immediate family. Honestly, I thought my uncle would have been our savior or at least found someone who could help my family survive that nightmare.

My heart was broken.

It felt like life was leaving my body. I began to feel the blow to the head. There was an instant downcast in David's eyes. I could tell that the guys instantly felt empowered now. They had so much to say.

"He don't care about you; he told us to do what we gotta do. Your own uncle doesn't care about your life." They laughed and taunted.

All I could do was cry. Hysterically. I cried harder at that moment than I had ever cried in my life. I felt more pain in that moment than I'd ever felt in my life. It was like I was preparing to die, and my family was preparing to die.

I have such a large family that expressed their love for me all the time, but those guys made me feel like I was alone because that one phone call would change our lives forever. I could have gotten better results if I called my grandmother or someone that I knew would risk their own life to save mine. A person that actually loved me! Why David urged me to call him I will never know.

♡

David's body got weaker and weaker. His loss of strength was probably partially due to the disappointing phone call. My poor baby girl didn't have a thing to eat or drink and she still seemed to be calm. Casually, I looked up and noticed we were headed back to our house.

"Call Bobby," David said.

I dialed the number and gave David the phone.

That was our last hope!

Bobby answered the phone and David was half yelling, half pleading "HELP ME PIMP, HELP ME!"

Bobby couldn't understand who was on the phone because he didn't recognize David's voice. David's voice was not his normal tone; he was in a lot of pain and exhausted.

Bobby hung up the phone!

I frantically called Bobby back at David's prompting.

When he picked up the phone, I was screaming, "WE NEED HELP!"

I didn't say what I said to my uncle. I was straight to the point.

"What's going on?" Bobby asked.

"We need help!" I repeated.

He said, "Okay, come to the house."

"Put it on the porch in a bag," I blurted out. Then I hung up.

We were about ten minutes away from his house. I don't know what time it was so I could have been making calls at inopportune times. It could have been too early to call or if they could have been too busy to answer. Yet, Bobby didn't hesitate to try to help my family. I felt confident in the call to him. Our family and his had become close. I don't think words can explain how I felt. For sure, Bobby was going to save my family and we would live to share the story of how grateful we were. I was so relieved by the sound of his voice saying those few words. "Come on, come on Tink!"

I hung up with Bobby and told David the good news. We approached the street that our friend lived on. Happiness and anxiety riddled my body at the same time. The kidnappers instructed that I would be the one to exit the van and retrieve what Booby had for us. I was given precise directions to follow when I got out of the van. I was not to go into the house. I was to just get what he had for us and come right back.

When we pulled up to the door, Bobby was waiting for us in the doorway. We were so close when I called Bobby that he didn't have time to really think or make any calls to help us. There was no time to call for backup.

Humiliated, I stood at Bobby's door and frantically explained what we needed: $150,000. The same amount I was told to tell my uncle. He then ran up the stairs to get what he had for us. He handed over the bag of money to me. He quickly told me there was about $40,000 in the bag.

POW! POW! POW! POW!

Before Bobby and I knew what was happening, the van screeched off at lightning speed.

"Justice! David! NO!"

I fell to the floor between the doorway and the porch. The money flew everywhere from the fall. Bobby picked me up off the floor and held me because I was so weak and limp. I couldn't get it together for the life of me at that point. I started to blackout.

Bobby spoke with his wife to let her know what was going on. She told him to give me some pants and a shirt to wear. Everything was moving super-fast. I was having an out of body experience. At some point, someone called the police. All I can remember is pacing back and forth in the street.

When the police arrived at Bobby's house, they told us the van was found at our home and they were going to take me back there. When I got there, I wasn't sure what was going on. The van was there, and the police were there, but no answers were given to me. I asked about my family and all they told me was that someone would be over to talk to me.

Finally, someone handed me my baby Justice.

Thank God!

She was untouched by those flying bullets that we heard. I was able to hug her and kiss her. All I could do was cry. Tears of joy fell uncontrollably from my eyes.

"Where's David?! What about David?!" I demanded to know once I had inspected Justice to ensure she wasn't hurt.

No one would give me any answers. I naively assumed that he was fine, and they were questioning him. They transported Justice and me to the Wilkinsburg police station for routine questioning. I was trying to get myself together, but in the meantime, I wanted to call Dana. I needed to let someone know what happened to us. I knew her number by heart because we spent a lot of time together. I was directed to a phone at the police station. Even though I was in tears, she instantly recognized my voice and she said the worst thing she could have ever said to me.

"TINK, what's going on? I'm at your house and there is a coroner's truck here!"

I just lost it at that point.

David was dead. She didn't have to say anymore. David. Was. Gone.

He had passed away all alone. No one was there with him to hold his hand. The man that gave so much, to everyone, was alone when he passed.

♡

I don't know who called her or when, but my mom made it to Pittsburgh from Ohio. I needed her so desperately. I needed her to make me feel safe. Better yet, I needed her to make me feel loved. My mom is that kind of mom. She can ask me what's wrong and I will break down and cry. That's the kind of relationship we have. She just knows.

We ended up at my grandmother's house surrounded by my support system. I mean everyone I could think of was stopping by to make sure we were okay. I just continued to leak tears.

I wanted to be close to David's mom so badly or even just talk to her, but she lived out of state. My heart ached for her because she lost her son. Even though I lost my guy, a mother's love was first. She and I were really close, and I could not wait to talk to her about what happened to our perfect family. When I was finally able to speak with her, she asked me if it was true and I confirmed that it was. We both just held the phone and cried. Eventually, we exchanged a few more words and she said that she would be in Pittsburgh just as soon as she could from Georgia. I would have done anything to get her there just to feel her touch. I wanted to hug her so I could feel a piece of him. As we finished up our heart to heart conversation, she asked, "Tink where is the money?"

Did this lady just ask me where some money is?!

When I didn't respond, she asked again.

"Tink where is the money?"

My fiancé, my daughter's father, HER SON has just died...was just MURDERED. My favorite guy. The nerve of her! We'd been awakened out of our sleep, kidnapped, beaten, and mentally broken down! David was DEAD!

I was heartbroken that she wanted to ask me something like that and all I wanted was my man and for us to comfort each other in our loss.

"TO HELL WITH THAT MONEY!!" I think I yelled. "If I had some money to give those guys, I would have given it and your son would still be alive. Secondly, if there was some money that money would be for me and my kids, not you!"

It's funny how death can bring out the worst in a person. Our relationship was forever changed from that moment on. I still respected her when we encountered one another, but the love I once had for her was gone. I have tried to be in contact with her since his passing, but it never lasts. I'm almost certain that it's because David is no longer with us. My daughter doesn't cry or get upset about not being able to be in contact with her grandmother and others. It's like we are so used to adjusting to people leaving out of our lives. It's not a good thing but it's true. We have learned to adjust, sometimes not so well.

Soon after that devastating phone call with David's mom, I received a visit at my grandmother's house. My uncle came in to see me. Yes, *that* uncle! He didn't even ask if I was okay. He didn't come out of concern for me at all. He came out of concern for himself and his family. He came to ask me if those kidnappers knew who he was or if they knew where he lived. He was only concerned about himself! My uncle spoke to me with no sensitivity or compassion. He wanted to talk about why he chose to do what he did to me, David and Justice. He was there to explain why he chose to say, "Do what you have to do." He wanted to remind me at a time like that that he turned his back on my family. He wasn't there to support me or hug me and my fatherless child. He was there to try to justify his actions. And whichever way you slice it, it will never be right.

As if my heart wasn't already broken into a million pieces.

> *This guy really had the nerve to talk to me about something like this after he slammed the phone down in our ears.*

I didn't have it in me to release the venom that was stirring inside me for him. He had cost David his life and almost cost us our lives!

I told him the truth that I didn't share any of his info with the guys and his family didn't have anything to worry about on account of me. I felt like I was dying inside even more. My protector wasn't there anymore to protect me from a man that was hurting me.

> *How could he do this to me? I'm his niece. His third born niece. So, I'm not just a distant family member. I thought he loved me enough to care about my well-being. But he didn't.*

Chapter Three

David's father allowed me to participate in planning his homegoing service. I really appreciated him for including me. I was his fiancée, but because we were not married yet, I had no right to any decisions.

I was still very much out of it. I was not able to concentrate but I tried to keep it together. Looking back, I wish my faith was as strong then as it is today. I don't remember being faithful. I know I would have had more peace.

His cousin Terry helped me pick out his suit for the service. We went to a few different stores in the North Hills area. We ended up at the mall for the final suit. Let me be honest here. If I asked Terry if the suit that I picked out for David was nice he would probably say, "Stinky Tinky, quit playing." I had to shake my head on that memory. David was a sharp dresser, as well as Terry. So, if anyone was going to have the final say it was going to be Terry even though he made me feel like I picked it out. Finding attire for David's service seemed to take forever. We held up well, but many tears fell from our eyes a few times. We didn't want to be there picking out clothes for his funeral! But we did it. We both wanted to make sure that David was still sharper than a tack in his casket. The way that man looked when he put clothes on...oh man! He could wear pretty much anything. He looked so good in a suit, but he also looked so good dressed down. One of his favorite tennis shoes to wear were Reebok classic high tops. The black and white ones with a fresh Lacoste collar shirt and khakis. He was a man that loved different flavors, so he could be caught wearing a super bright shirt or your basic tans. Either way he was going to catch your eye.

♡

I loved my hairdresser on the north side. She always made me feel like I was welcomed. I felt like it was okay that I wasn't from that side of town. I felt safe with her. Lord knows that if you ain't from over there you may have it rough. David and I talked about her doing my hair for our wedding. I wanted Ms. Kim to put my hair in a classy bun off to the right side of my head. So, when I wore my short, classy, white veil that came over my eyes down to my chin, it would hit just right. Almost like a hat style. Instead, Ms. Kim had to give me a different look because I had to bury him. I wanted to represent him in the most respectful way. Not that it was hard to do because I always carried myself in a humble, respectful lady-like way. I wanted her to do my hair how Angela Bassett's hair was in *Waiting to Exhale* before she cut it all off and kicked him to the curb. I felt like she looked so elegant when her hair was long and straight back.

Days passed and we were getting closer to the funeral. Friends and family started coming over and showing more and more love. I have always had a loving family and great support from my friends and their families. The gathering house at the time was my Mom-Mom's house. So, all the food, cards, hugs and kisses were coming over there. I don't think I ever got tired of it. I embraced it as much as I could because when it was over, I was left with my thoughts and I had to face the worst all over again--my dreams and the what-ifs about those cowards who were still on the loose.

What if they would come back while we slept? What if they were going to try and kill me now?

We never went back to our home because I couldn't fake that I was okay doing life without David. That was *our* home and he was not there with me. That was way too much reality in my face at one time. Justice and I would be staying at Mom-Mom's until further notice. Whenever further notice was. I had many sleepless nights. I didn't want to miss a beat. I wanted to be more alert if anyone wanted to try to invade my space again. Even at my grandmother's house, I worried if they would try to come and finish the job. It was kind of hard to sleep not knowing why any of it happened and who sent them. The unknowing kept me up plenty of nights. I can be honest; I was very afraid.

There were so many people and so much food coming and going daily that a lot of it was a blur. I wish I could remember everyone who was there so I could personally thank them for loving on me and supporting us. Ms. Kim touched my heart in such a big way in the short time we knew each other. Not only did she come over with a card, but she brought food and sat for hours to make sure I was okay. I was able to hear her talk about a few stories about David. She shared with me how he would always come into the shop making jokes. She also told me that she knew that he loved me. I was happy for the time with her. I am forever grateful.

♡

It felt like it was an all-day affair.

David would have wanted everyone to see him in his sharp suit.

I remember arriving at the funeral home early with the family. I was ready to go check out my man. I was missing him so much. This was the longest I had been away from him since we met. He was dressed to a T. He most certainly was. He was laying there so handsome and looking at peace. I mean it looked like his soul was resting perfectly. I know this was his wake, but I wanted to see him as much as I could. I was able to talk with him before people came in. I cried and laughed a little at some of the things I said to him. Between him and I of course.

I stood at the casket the entire time. You hear me? The whole time in 4-inch classy heels. I didn't move from him. Not to pee, nothing. Thank God that I had my family and friends there to help keep me together. They were able to help keep Justice occupied. They made sure that she was occupied but also distracted from what her mom was going through. Every so often I would get some love from her hugs and kisses.

I couldn't tell you where I got that strength from back then, but I know now that it was the grace of God. I mean I didn't have much energy to start with and I wasn't eating so how in the heck did I stand for all those hours? It was almost like I was on a spiritual fast. Besides the love and support from my family and friends, I know that was nothing but God sustaining me. I remember hearing that David's wake looked like a celebrity's wake from the outside. There were so many people there to see the man that I loved. He was such a loving and caring person so I wouldn't expect anything less.

The morning of the service, we were all getting ready at my Mom-Mom's house. There were so many of us in the house. My family came up from York, so the go-to places were always my house and Mom-Mom's house. Since we weren't going to my house, we were all with Mom-Mom. I was getting ready in slow motion. The Valium had kicked in already. I finally decided to take it so that I would be able to maintain a calm demeanor. I'm not one to take pills so I really didn't trust that I could be in control of my actions that day. Not that I wanted to harm anyone; I just didn't want to break down and not be able to see the service through to the end.

We were all dressed in the same colors. I wore tan and cream as did Justice and David. As I began to put my pants suit on, I started to cry but no sound came out. It was the deepest, hurtful cry I ever experienced. I don't think words could ever explain this cry. I eventually pulled myself together so I could finish putting the final touches on our baby girl. She was dressed like she was a flower girl. She was such a beautiful baby with her beauty mark on her forehead. She wore a cream dress with a little bit of gold sparkle on it and gold and cream hair balls to match. I was such a mess that day that I couldn't do Justice's hair. Britney would always hook her hair up so pretty, and she did that morning as well.

Before we left to say goodbye to David, I was trying to get myself together to talk to Justice about what was about to take place at the church and graveyard. As much as I tried to think of a conversation to have with my 15-month-old baby, I knew she wouldn't be able to understand. My first thought was to say, *"Baby, you know mommy and daddy love you right?"* Her response would be to give me a kiss as tears fall down my face.

Then I would say, *"Daddy loves you so much that he wanted to protect you from anything or anyone that would bring harm to you."*

That's when I realized that she wouldn't be able to understand any of what I was saying. She's 15 months. I barely understood why it was happening.

As I looked in the mirror before we went out the door, I realized that would be our final time dressing alike. David and I did that often. We once attended our friend's graduation party. The instructions were to wear your favorite sports team. So, we did. We both wore the 76ers. I got a jersey made into a dress. David had on leather shorts. We were so cute.

"This is it David," I said to myself.

The homegoing service for David was such a blur. Seeing him lying in the casket was so hard for me. I know that funerals are hard for people. I get that. But, knowing that he was laying there and never ever going to wake up and greet me was too much! I remember drifting off into deep thought often. I was in such deep thought I can't remember much of anything about the service. I don't know if the preacher said my name correctly or if it went by smoothly, who attended or who didn't. It was almost like a fog I was in or a dream that I was just floating along.

No, it was a nightmare. I was living a nightmare.

Chapter Four

The healing process that I had to go through when David first left our family was so painful. I had so many adult decisions to make and I was still so young. I was only 21 years old. I had to make all the calls for my life and a one-year-old, ALONE.

I'd gone from my mom's care to David's care. He took care of so much for our family, and we never talked about what we'd do if we were apart because we were never apart.

Now what? How is this even possible? David took care of most of the paperwork that made our lives run smoothly. He shared a lot of it with me, but he was the one who made the calls and handled all the details. I knew how because he taught me, but I knew whatever he was doing was right and if not, he would fix. Whenever we purchased vehicles, he did the talking but he would have me right there with him so I could actually see what was going on. He would always say, 'just in case you want to buy me a car one day.' And he knew I would if I was able.

The voices in my head were overwhelming.

Should I stay in the beautiful home that David worked so hard on for us, without him? And if I did would I be able to handle being there seeing and smelling him every moment of my day? Will those criminals try to come back to our home to finish the job that they started because I was the only witness? What was I to do about these major life choices that I had to make within a matter of days?

Those voices helped me with my next move. It looked like my daughter and I were not staying in our home that her dad worked so hard to make a home for us. I was still scared for my life and my family and friends were also concerned. Everyone involved in my life in a major way was pushing for me to return to Ohio with my mom and stepdad. All the 'what if' questions were circling around even more. The answers consistently were, 'You cannot go back to your house. You just can't and you won't want to anyway now that David isn't with you.' They were right.

I picked up my life and moved to Ohio with my mom. I was uneasy because the thugs that came into our home and disrupted our lives were still out in this crazy world. With our faces, home, and cars being plastered on the news for days there was no way that I would have peace stuck in Pittsburgh. My family and I asked the detectives handling our case if it was okay for Justice and me to move. They reassured me that it was fine and if I was able to do that; they also believed that was best. They had all the information they needed from me at that time and when necessary they would call me with any updates. They were confident that this case was going to be solved.

♡

My mom took charge and made it all happen. We got a moving truck and headed to our new life with no head of household, but a 21-year-old girl raising a baby as a single parent.

I wish it were Beverly Hills but Ohio, here we come.

My family in Ohio made us feel so welcomed. Sometimes it felt like we would be okay. We had family gatherings and plenty of laughs all the time. My cousins and I would stay up late and laugh for hours. I had such a good time. I truly love and appreciate them for taking us under their wings.

Then there were times when it felt like my life was over. I wanted to stay in bed for days. My body was very fatigued, and I wasn't trying to do anything about it. I just wanted to stay in bed and sleep. Eating wasn't a priority. I was able to do a lot of sleeping because I was staying with my parents. They picked up a lot of the slack with Justice for weeks that turned into months.

There would be some not so good days, hours and moments. I couldn't go out anywhere or do anything without crying. I would try my hardest not to cry or get into my feelings. I remember being at Friday's restaurant down on Mayfield Road with Justice, my mom, and Chris. I had to run to the bathroom and let it all out. I saw a couple with their child and just the sight of a complete family together triggered my thoughts of what I had lost. What Justice lost. What *we* lost.

When I was a kid growing up, the girls would talk about how we saw the future. They gushed over what colleges they would attend. I did as well, but I was just acting like I wanted to attend Indiana University of Pittsburgh (IUP). I even had it printed under my yearbook picture. In reality, all I ever wanted was a family. I wanted to have a husband, about five kids, a white picket fence, a red front door, and a dog that my husband and kids took care of. Yes, five kids! Being an only child, I wanted my kids to have someone to be there for them. David and I had planned on having a big house full of kids, always having food cooked and food in the fridge for when they had company. I was so happy that we had the same dreams. My life was finally coming together. We met and fell in love, got engaged, bought a house, had a baby and next was marriage and relocating.

But that was all over.

It took me a very long time to heal in so many areas. My heart broke into a million pieces when I lost David. He was my best friend. I was lost, and I felt ashamed, broken, and damaged. I was what I dreaded the most. A single parent at 21. Hell, I wanted five kids or more with this man, and now it was taken away from me. No more dreaming with him aloud. My dreams were now over.

All I saw in my family and around me were broken families. Dads who were no longer present because the parents could not co-parent together for whatever reason and they had given up on being under the same roof. I saw mothers struggling, working two jobs to make ends meet. Their kids grew up too fast to stay home alone while these single moms went to their second jobs. I saw plenty of strong single parents that I truly admired, but in my eyes, being a single parent mostly meant hardship and struggle. I didn't want that for my own kids. I wanted to get as close to perfect as possible. I wanted my own family. My own happy family. *Why is this dream so hard to come true in the world that we live in?* We wanted to give our kids what we never really had. Yes, we had stepparents, but it wasn't the same. We always just wanted to love on as many kids as we could.

My precious daughter. My Justice! I was so broken for her. My thoughts skipped town.

> *How am I going to tell her that her hands-on father is not coming home to give her a bath or have daddy-daughter time? No more dropping her off at Ms. Penny's daycare and Justice looking forward to him picking her up. How is my baby girl going to get through her days when it's time for the father-daughter dance? And who is going to give her that daddy love that only daddies can give?*

I mean I had two stepfathers, but I don't know what it is like to have a dad that belonged to *me*. David was that father to Justice and our kids. Now, he was gone because of those cowards.

One Halloween, my mom, Justice and I sitting on the front porch at her house in Cleveland waiting to take Justice trick-or-treating. Justice was dressed up as Tinkerbell that year.

Go figure. Some man walked up the street and out of nowhere, Justice said, "Is that my daddy, Grandma?" I tell you, that about broke my already fragile heart once again. We explained to her that her dad was in heaven. Justice then screamed, "Heaven come get me!" My baby girl wanted her dad desperately and so did I. But there wasn't anything I could do to help either one of us. That moment led me further into a deep depression.

There was no one else in my life that had gone through what I was going through. Not even close to what I experienced. Therefore, getting help with coping from a loved one was out of the question. Looking back, I must say things could have been a lot worse but that was the worst for me. I know with the pain that weighed heavily on my heart I could have easily got involved in drugs or some other kind of coping mechanism. But my ways of grieving were different. I lost my appetite and weight. Imagine that. I was already small and lost more weight. I was easily 110 pounds, 5 feet 6 inches but I look taller because of my long legs. So, I looked skinnier than I really was. My grandad told me a few times that my face was skinny or looked sunk in. Indeed, it was, but I didn't notice because I wasn't paying attention to myself. Instead, God positioned me with people that I know loved me or would grow to love me. People that could see me and help me see myself. A few of those people suggested therapy but I didn't act on it right away. Some people suggested it because they felt I should get another prescription to help me cope. And that was one of the main reasons I stayed away.

I know that therapy is taboo with black people. A lot of us are taught early on that you don't talk to folks about 'family business.' If they do see a therapist, they ain't talking about it. It's looked at as a sign of weakness. But I was trying to save my life. So, I went to therapy.

Finding a therapist wasn't easy. I went to several doctors trying to find the right one which meant sharing my story over again each time so they could help me in the way that I needed. That process was a roller coaster ride all by itself. I stopped after I saw two people. Both wanted to prescribe pills and I wasn't taking anyone's drugs. I know different needs for different people, but I wasn't comfortable with it. Instead, I went to therapy and I partied. That's how I coped. I was 21 and trying to figure out how to make it through. Therapy didn't last long. Either I wasn't focused, or I didn't feel like it was working anymore or the ones I went to weren't giving me what I felt I needed. Thus, I stopped going. I depended on myself, family, and drinking.

My numbing medicine was drinking. Hennessy straight, no chaser! Straight to the point. Sad to say, but I had so much fun drinking and laughing. It wasn't every day or anything, but it was the new me for about two years. I was never a drinker because I was underage. It wasn't anything that I was used to so when I started drinking it was different. It helped me get through the pain of what only I was going through. I didn't go in thinking I needed something to get through the day; it just happened. I never put myself in a place to be disrespected or anything. The people that I was around knew what I was going through. No judgments from them.

I had some great times with my Ohio sisters and brothers. Just to name a few (*In my DMX voice*) There was Aaricka, Dawn, Denise, Precious, Stephanie, Ciara, Joli, Jessica, Christian, Candice, Alonzo, Dontae, Bob, Tee, Nikki, Ben and so many more. I love these guys so much. Each one of them, named and unnamed, holds a special place in my heart. I can't thank them enough. OMG, I can think of so many funny moments that we shared together. I remember being at Carolina's with Precious and Steph. That's when Blackberry phones were popping. I was feeling good and I heard this phone ring and of course, I was thinking it was mine. Well, I politely asked this man if he could change his ringtone. Who do I think I am to ask this man that? But it was funny at the time. Precious still cracks up about that.

We had a favorite meeting place called The Touch of Italy. It's a small place to meet up with good people and have something good to eat. Oh, and play the jukebox. I loved playing DJ on the jukebox. We'd take turns feeding the machine so we could hear our favorite music. It may have been about four or five of us that would go regularly. The Touch of Italy felt like the TV show *Cheers*, where everyone knows your name. Only my name was Pittsburgh. They called me Pittsburgh because of course, I had to always talk my trash about the Steelers. It wouldn't be right if I didn't even though I knew very little about football. Good nights and laughter in this place.

We were going to hang out at the Touch one night and my girl Steph told me that she wanted me to meet someone. He didn't live in Ohio, but he was there often, which meant he had business there and lived there a good bit of the time. She felt that we would get along great. Steph thought our personalities would mesh well. He literally jumped on a plane from California and came to Ohio. That was interesting because neither of us knew what to expect but we weren't necessarily concerned. Joe walked in The Touch full of life. 6 feet, 4inches, shoulders out, dark and handsome with a beautiful smile. Geez! I wasn't ready! He was built like a football player. We exchanged numbers and kept in contact after that night.

One time we were all at Steph's house to bring in the new year. We were all single and decided to bring in the new year together with our kids. The kids were upstairs, and the adults were downstairs. Well, we were having fun dancing, eating and, of course, drinking. Everyone knows that Ohio folks love to dance and so do I, even if I can't really dance. I'm sure Precious was singing. Her voice is so pretty, and she isn't afraid to share it. I had so much fun that night. Joe was also in town. He was a little older than us but cool as heck. He came to the house party to bring in the new year with us. No one should be alone on New Year's Eve. Joe was like a science project. He shared with me that he had never had a drink or smoked anything in his life. That didn't seem normal or real. With the world that we live in, I wondered how he escaped without trying anything once. Now, I don't speak from a lot of experience of engaging in the festivities but, *never*? I loved that quality about him. So, there we were bringing in the new year and he was super sober, and I was having a grand time drinking and dancing with my new family.

We were enjoying each other so much that after the party was over, we left to go to my apartment to get clothes for me to wear to the Browns' football game the next afternoon. We went back to his home to sleep. The houses in his neighborhood were what a girl like me only dreamed of as a kid. I mean every house on the street was huge. I could not believe that his house was situated with those mansions. I thought my home in Pittsburgh was something special, but my walk-up jacuzzi tub didn't have anything on what I saw that night. The living area was open with big windows and the cars were definitely out of my price range. I found out that his cousin was a player on the team. The next day, I had my first experience attending a professional NFL game with someone that actually knew the person playing on the team. We entered through the family entrance. That was exciting; no waiting in long lines or searching for a parking space. That definitely made a girl feel special.

Even though I was hungover, that man took care of me. And once again, there was no judgment. He could have easily looked at me as less than because every time he saw me it seemed like a happy hour. I mean, I was far from an alcoholic, but I was doing some drinking. I went from celebrating the ball dropping just a few hours prior to being at a stadium enjoying a football game. Joe pulled out all the stops too! We pulled right up to the stadium where valet greeted us and parked our vehicle in the who's who parking under the stadium. It was just the Browns that we were going to see, but then it wasn't just the Browns. It was me getting a glimpse of where my life could go and that I could have better. I could be happy again.

I'd been in Ohio for almost two years and was finally trying to live again. People were working hard to keep me together from going down a dark road with thoughts of my past and Joe was, sure enough, helping me keep my mind off the bad. Initially, I questioned myself about our friendship though. *Was he with me just because he wanted something to do while in Ohio or did this man really enjoy his time with me?*

♡

Joe and I had been kicking it for a while. I went to work and when I got off, I went to handle my mommy duties, hang out with the family, and put Justice to bed. Afterward, I left to hang out with Joe until morning. I had no clue where our relationship was going, or if it was going anywhere. While I was getting to know him, Justice would stay with my mom and Chris. I didn't want to bring her around just yet. Joe and I never had the conversation about becoming one, but we really enjoyed each other's company. He was from California, living here during the football season but also flying in and out to see me often. So, seeing him wasn't an issue. We did a lot of things together. On one of our first dates, we went to the movies. When I went to open the car door, he told me not to touch the handle. *Okay!* I didn't. I wasn't sure what was going on, but I obeyed. When we arrived at the movies, I again went to open the door to the theatre, and he smacked my hand. *What is going on here?* He then told me that it's a man's job to open the door. He meant what he was saying. I never touched a door again with that gentleman.

I know that we fell in love with each other. We did so much together--movies, Dave & Busters and of course, lots of eating. One day Joe decided to switch things up. We went to the grocery store and got stuff to cook at home. We purchased all the ingredients to make tacos and for dessert I planned to bake a chocolate cake with chocolate icing. I could not believe that I was about to get down and cook in his kitchen. Even though they were just tacos, I was about to make it all taste like it was fine dining in that fancy kitchen. Soft and hard shell tacos coming up!

I didn't grow up with any type of wealth. My mom was a single, young parent and didn't teach me anything about financial literacy. She did what she could, which was a lot. The only thing that I saw growing up was the latest up and coming drug dealer with many cars who had to watch his back because of the police and multiple girls. So, I thought that was as good as it got. I always knew I wanted a better life, but I darn sure didn't think it would be with this type of man. Even though he made me feel great and loved on me by any means, he didn't come off with an "I'm better than you" attitude.

I struggled to see how our situation could turn into something great. Perhaps, it was due to my limited mindset. He offered something that I always wanted, something that I was deserving of. However, I was in such a broken place that I didn't think that I was worthy enough to be with a man that once played professional football and lived a wealthy lifestyle with big houses and fancy cars. I didn't think a regular person from Pittsburgh and no college degree could have ever come close to a man as well-spoken

with lavish material possessions like Joe. I didn't see myself
as someone good enough, partly because of what happened
on the day that changed my life, but also because I wasn't
educated in the traditional sense. I never dreamed of
anything for myself other than having a family one day and
taking care of that family. Maybe because I didn't see it
growing up, I didn't know that a better life existed. I didn't
know that people like Joe and his cousin just worked really
hard and built their wealth from nothing.

The day finally came for Joe to meet my Justice. She was
about 3 years old at the time. We hung out for a few hours
at his house and watched tv and talked with Justice. It was a
nice feeling for me to be able to play house for a few hours.
If only for a sliver in time, I was able to escape my reality of
sadness, depression, and loneliness.

As eye-opening as my relationship with Joe was, I couldn't
maintain it. Even though it felt like it was years of knowing
him, it was short-lived. My insecurities were the demise of
the relationship. Everything that I knew I wasn't made me
believe that I was not worthy of the love that Joe wanted to
so freely give me. When I looked at our stark differences, I
could not fathom a future with him. I did not come from
money; Joe was an ex-professional football player. I was
uneducated; Joe had a degree. I just did not measure up and
that made me uncomfortable. It's safe to say that I
sabotaged that good thing all because of my toxic thinking.

To this day, Joe and I remain great friends. Many years after
our romantic relationship ended, I shared my truth with
him. He wished that I had told him much earlier so that he

could have eased my concerns. Open and honest communication is truly the fiber of any relationship.

Chapter Five

Living in Ohio was a great place for me to deal with the reality that I still didn't have any closure with what happened to David because, years later, those cowards were still on the run. I needed somewhere safe to raise my daughter, but it wasn't fair that we had to miss out on so much because they chose to be evil. There were many family functions that we weren't able to attend, not because we weren't invited but because I was still fearful. The thoughts of my life possibly being interrupted again was unimaginable. So, we opted out of the family functions.

Finally, I got the call.

After two years of waiting, the criminals were finally caught for the crimes they committed! Two of the guys were in custody. It was the best news I heard in a long time. I know that only two guys were in custody but that was better than none. I was given so much information that I really didn't have to ask any questions. The detectives were hoping the two men in custody would lead them to the others involved in our abduction.

They continued the investigation as promised and were able to take it to court. As several court proceedings approached, I became more and more uneasy.

> *Should I go, should I not go? Am I strong enough to deal with this? What if these guys have a Mafia-type power behind them that they can come and do something to me, and my daughter won't have either one of her parents? Or worse, my mom loses both of us this time.*

There was so much going on in my head.

I felt so hopeless. So weak. So alone. The only person I wanted more than anything was dead! I just wanted to scream so many times. I still couldn't believe I was the person who was taken out of her bed against her will, robbed of so much and still expected to go on with life and had to testify against those animals.

> *Why me? But why not me? Why did He choose to allow me to go through this?*

I wish I knew the scripture back then, "I can do all things through Christ who strengthens me..." I know that's the only reason I got through that. Because of His strength in me.

Part of me is reluctant to share this part of my life but then another part wants to be as transparent as possible. I want to encourage you to choose to keep going. Better yet, I want to push you to keep the faith. Overwhelming pain still comes as if it were just last week. I don't feel that I can truly get away from this tragic event that I call my past because it lives with me every day. As I tear up now, my stomach begins to ache because it still feels like a fresh wound that continues to paralyze me repeatedly. Sometimes without warning. That makes my daily fight so much harder. This fight to stay sane or afloat sometimes feels like I won't ever be normal again. Then I realize that I am normal. We all are. We all have our own paths. Our own stories. This was a part of my path. A part of my story.

Having to face those animals and their families in that courtroom and having to keep my emotions intact because I was told that the judge frowns on outbursts from both sides was unbearable. I wanted to walk up to them and punch them repeatedly until I felt better and then punch them some more.

I felt like I had the weight of the world on my shoulders as I sat in that courtroom. I had to be a woman first and keep it together. My feelings had to be put aside while I took care of my business so we could get justice for David. The amount of stress and anxiety that I experienced was crazy. I was constantly looking over my shoulder. Being extra careful. Scared to go see my family. Scared to bring or leave my daughter with other people.

I was scared to live.

I didn't ask for any of this.

Those guys took away my sense of peace all in one morning, in just a few short hours.

I had to take Justice back and forth with me from Cleveland to Pittsburgh. While I attended the court appearances, she played in the courthouse's childcare room. Justice was always such a peaceful baby and a well-behaved little girl. I recall one time when my stress level was through the roof. I had to leave her with complete strangers so I could go handle non-traditional mommy duties. For a moment, I relived a Lifetime movie where a person had to leave their baby in a court daycare and went back and the baby was gone missing. Justice was in the playroom and I was called down because she had an accident. She peed on herself. She was about 3 years old at the time and had been fully potty-trained for some time. My baby never had any type of accident - not even when she was being potty trained. She'd never even wet the bed, not one time. It was almost like she was a perfect baby in that area but not that day. She had an accident. The only thing that I could assume was that she could sense that something wasn't right. I went to get my baby and just cried with her.

After enduring grueling testimony and reliving the terror of that night as I sat on the stand, justice was served. On Monday, April 25, 2005, the two men that I identified and testified against were sentenced to life in prison. As anyone can imagine, this part of the story is painful for me to write even 15 years later.

I recall one of those reality TV stars telling someone to Google her because they wanted to know who she was and what she did. Now, I find it remarkably interesting that I am actually Googleable too!

Part Two

DREAMING NEW DREAMS

Chapter Six

While Joe and I were still dating and I was living in Cleveland, I let Justice stay a few days with my cousin, Likah, after we all attended a family reunion in Pittsburgh. Likah asked if Justice could stay with her for a couple of days. When the visit was over, I snuck into the city to pick her up. I did not want to see anyone or be seen. My cousin was living up East Hills at the time. After visiting for a while with my family, Justice and I left Likah's house, and my attempt to dodge anyone was unsuccessful. I ran into a familiar face.

It was Mister. Mister had shown some interest before and tried to talk to me several times over the years. I ran into him once when I was in high school, but we never got a chance to kick it because I was very inexperienced when it came to doing the things that he wanted to do. I was still very immature about a lot of things. When I saw him that day, it still wasn't time because I was figuring out life after David.

I remember writing in my diary about Mister: '*Mister wants to go to the hotel this weekend but he's moving way too fast.*' Yea, that wasn't happening.

At that point, we lost contact with each other. Then I saw him a few years later for NBA All-Star weekend in Atlanta, Georgia. We were at the airport, both returning to Pittsburgh. He once again expressed how he wanted to get to know me, but I was engaged to be married and had just had a baby. He told me he would see me on the porch often. I assumed that he was in the area often because I was always home. When I was with David, I had tunnel vision. It was about him and our family.

As I picked up Justice, he drove past and spotted me. He never got out of his truck, but we exchanged numbers. We began to call each other often. What started as short conversations to check in slowly turned into talking multiple times a day for hours. It seemed like we were getting closer through our long talks. I guess I felt like because we had crossed paths a few times throughout the years that I somehow *knew* him and that I could possibly trust him. Still going through the grieving process, I'm sure that wasn't thinking properly. Not because he was a bad guy but because I needed more 'me' time. Time to sort things out for me. I had just fallen in love with that beautiful male specimen from California and there I was talking to a familiar face from Pittsburgh.

> *What am I doing? I love Joe but he doesn't know it and he hasn't told me he loves me yet either. I don't know how to handle this. I have not ever been in a situation like this. Mister and I are getting closer and closer with each other and now I'm handling the situation with Joe all wrong.*

It seemed like the distance between Joe and I grew further and further apart. I don't know if it was him being in Cali more due to the football season being over or if it was me talking to Mister more. It wasn't an ugly break up, but the distance just started to take a toll on the relationship. Maybe he felt the change in me and opted to give me space.

In my heart I believe I chose to continue to keep in contact with Mister because he was familiar and he was moving the conversation to another level, asking for more time and asking to come visit. Plus, that lie continued to play in my head on repeat; I wasn't good enough for Joe. I was thinking that Mister was kind of what I deserved. Although, I loved the new vision of possibly starting a life with Joe. I could move further away from my past and have a fresh start. Moving to California sounded like a great idea! Who in their right mind would give up sunny Cali for lake effect snowy Ohio? Me. I did. All because I still thought less than myself. I don't recall any last words with Joe, but the love spell was over. At least for that moment.

♡

Mister started to come to see me almost every weekend in Ohio. Sometimes he would get a hotel. Once we got closer, he stayed at my apartment. He spent time with my family and got to know my daughter. There wasn't a formal introduction right away because we were only friends. My mom and Chris had many get-togethers so keeping it low-key wasn't hard to pull off. I got so comfortable with Mister that I started going to visit him. I was not completely healed as my new relationship blossomed, but I was doing better.

Some days were better than others. For the most part, Mister made me feel safe. He offered me a sense of security that I would be fine because I was with him.

From that point, we were pretty much an item. He was the man I felt could save me from me. The man that could bring life back to this body of mine. The man that said, "I love you" in less than a month. I never questioned his love because I was feeling something as well.

I remember it like it was yesterday.

I was on lunch break sitting on the curb and he was taking a break as well. We talked so much on the phone; it was crazy, but it was a good crazy. After that it was on! I traveled to Pittsburgh and he came to Ohio. His daughter and Justice got along well, so she would have an older sister to bond with. It was unexpected, but he gave me a key to his house early on. He stepped up quickly to prove to me that he was ready for what I wanted, and our worlds were so ready to come together as one.

I don't know what or how it happened, but once we were together, I made the transition back to the city I thought I would never go back to. Mister changed that for me. We moved back to Pittsburgh and started our journey to live together as a family. Before I knew it, I was pregnant, and he asked to marry me on my birthday in 2007. It was a very thoughtful proposal. He wanted our kids to witness a man stepping up and doing the right thing. He was so happy to be able to finally live out the dream of having a wife and kids. I was happy that I was able to help give him a few of the things he wanted in life. While I was excited to become his wife, I was incredibly nervous. I talked to him several times and let him know that I wasn't sure if we were doing the right thing. The right thing I questioned was if we were supposed to be together. I didn't want to start a family with him if he wasn't sure we were what he really wanted.

I couldn't help but think about all that I had been through with David. He was there one day and then gone the next. Even though David and I planned to grow old together that didn't happen. I was scared to start over. Starting over wouldn't be with one child that time; it would be with two. Even though I didn't try to bring my past into the future, there was no way around it. David and Mister were on two different paths, but the one thing they had in common was their desire to plan a future with me. After Mister and I had a heart to heart conversation, I felt more comfortable with our decision. We decided to wait to get married until after our baby was born. I was able to bless him with a baby boy--his namesake. Mister was so happy to have a son. We had the full package and we were in our glory together.

We enjoyed making quick road trips to see different family members for family reunions or cookouts. Sometimes, we took road trips just to get away. One of my favorite family getaways was the family cruise to the Bahamas with my mom's side of the family. It was probably about twenty of us. Besides my seasickness and spending too much money on chocolate-covered strawberries, we had an amazing time. The kids had a blast too and of course, that included Mister's daughter. She and Justice were old enough to hang out without their parents, so they enjoyed that independence on the ship. Baby boy was not getting out of my sight though. Mister was able to come and go as he pleased on that ship, but I chose to stay with my baby. As always, I felt (*and knew*) that no one could take better care of my baby than me. This trip was a real joy for us all.

Soon he began to plan our wedding. I didn't have to do anything, and I was okay with that. I didn't care about any of that girly stuff. My primary concern lied with being happy and that was it. My life's desires changed so much throughout the years. Things that once seemed appealing to me were no longer priorities for me. I went from wanting to plan a cripped out wedding with Mitch to wanting to just go to the courthouse with David to not planning my own wedding with Mister. I was able to be myself--*so I thought*--with that man.

We had a double wedding with Mister's friend, who was also my son's godfather. He and his friend planned everything. I gave some input, but overall, it was like my own version of a Cinderella story. We all tied the knot in June of 2008. Mister and I were creating the life that we wanted. We both worked and saw each other off when we could. I worked for a good company that allowed me the opportunity to relocate to be with my family whenever we were ready to leave Pittsburgh. Mister and I had previously discussed that plan. The two of us were truly in our groove of marriage. Together, we did everything from planning family vacations to going grocery shopping. I planned the dinner and was grateful to cook for my family. Each day before my husband left for work at 5:00 am, I made him hot breakfast sandwiches and prepared his lunch. Yes, I was that kind of wife and I enjoyed every bit of it! I even woke up early on my off days to make hot a breakfast for my family. I really enjoyed being that mom and partner.

I felt like my dreams were finally back on track. All the kids that David and I fantasized about could still happen. Finally, I felt that sense of being safe and secure again. I had a newly secure marriage and I was convinced that the man I married was going to be the light that I so desperately needed. My son was going to have his father raising him in the same house, and my baby girl Justice had a shot on not missing out on having a daddy's love. I mean, come on, that's all I wanted for her. For her not to feel without. For her to know what it's like to have that protective man in her life. My daughter finally had a father on earth as well as in Heaven. Her new dad stepped right in and treated her like his biological child. Mister woke Justice up for school in the mornings and he made sure she was picked up from friends' houses. He ensured her safety whenever she left the house.

My favorite was when they attended the father-daughter dance together. I think I really loved him on a deeper level at that moment. The father-daughter dance is such a big deal. Consider the father-daughter dance at weddings. Unfortunately, I never had that type of dance, but I didn't expect my daughter to not be able to have it. But with Mister as a present force in her life, she wouldn't have to miss out. I was so excited for her to attend. Mister and I prepared everything for the dance. We planned to coordinate their outfits. On our shopping quest, we found the perfect lilac shirt to complement her dress of the same color. On the day of the dance, I took plenty of pictures to preserve great memories. When I saw them leave together for their date, tears of joy began to leak from my eyes. My heart was filled with so much gratitude and love. The love I felt for Mister that day was exuding from a different place than usual. It was a good feeling that I couldn't put into words.

I enjoyed every drop of my new life! My husband and I said, "I love you" at least twenty times a day. I was what you call happy!

♡

Everything was all good and then things began to take a turn.

I recall him telling me a few things about the lady who catered our baby shower. She tried to convince my husband and his mother that I wasn't good enough for him because of what I had been through.

Who is she to judge me for a situation that no one would ask for?

I never really got to know the lady but if I knew how she felt about me, I would have made other plans for my shower. My family cooks damn good! The food was good but if I had to be judged or looked down on, then my Mom, Aunt T, Pop Pop, Aunt Lisa, Aunt Frenchie, or whoever would have made my food. Heck even Ms. Sharon would have made me some of her white baked mac and cheese. For her to judge me without knowing much about me was not cool. Her past probably isn't all that clean, but that's not my business. Maybe she wanted my husband for herself or had someone else in mind for him. Maybe she should have spoken on that instead of discussing my kidnapping like that was something I signed up for. Furthermore, she had no clue that my husband wasn't a saint or what he was about to put me through. I'm not sure exactly how that affected his thoughts but I'm sure it gave him some ammo to boost his ego.

Do I not deserve to be loved or move on because of an event in my past?

Because I understand how traumatizing and unjust it is, I vow to never judge a person based on their past.

Shortly after those major events were over, the mental abuse started. It was obvious to those close to me before I realized it myself. People began to say things to me in front of him. Most were indirect comments, but some were very direct. His actions towards me were almost like I was scum, but then there were times when he wanted to be around me. I overlooked a lot of things because I didn't care. For instance, he would not let me drive any of the four trucks that he owned throughout our marriage. He really thought I wasn't good enough to drive his vehicles. I never cared to have a conversation with him about it because I was good with driving my own.

Why should I even have a conversation with him about something like this?

Clearly, he thought his actions were justified because he spoke about it to other people. I spoke about it too. My Uncle and I would have short, sweet talks about things that were going on. He would be so mad at me and tell me to make sure that I always had my own because '*that dude ain't ever gonna change!*'

I know that my husband loved me, but he certainly had his own strange way of showing it. I'm not mad at him now but I deserved so much more without demand.

Sometimes I felt that we had a perfect life then in the blink of an eye it felt like I was in a living hell. Every other week it was something different. It seemed like our happiness was based on how he was feeling. I had to feed off him. If he had a good day, then I had permission to have a good day too. I slowly began to slip back into such a dark place. I was losing who I was for sure. I thinned out more than I needed to be. Mister seemed to look happier than I could understand. I couldn't come out of depression for long.

Why wasn't he helping me when I knew he saw me hurting?

Little things started to add up. He hung out a bit too much and came home cocky and extra arrogant. As the old folks say, he was smelling himself. Mister was out acting like he was single. My gut felt something, but I couldn't pinpoint what.

Thankfully, our kids did not suffer through our toxic relationship. We did surprisingly good with keeping up appearances. One thing that I do regret is sometimes our fussing escalated and the kids would hear us. Those were certainly not my proudest moments. When things got too heated, one of us would leave to cool off.

I started to feel less than. My womanhood was being stripped away from me. Once again, I was battling thoughts that I was not good enough for my man. I felt like I wasn't worthy to be with him because he brought so much to the table. All I was good for was cooking and taking care of the kids. I didn't develop those thoughts overnight or alone. He made sure that it was known to me and others that he was the reason why things were going 'round. Mister was constantly reminding me of what he did for me and all that he purchased for me. He felt that if it wasn't for him, I would still be living in a situation that I didn't want to be in. I never ever acted like I did more than him, but he made me aware that what I was doing was not enough. I felt more alone in my marriage than I did when I was actually single and alone. Unbelievably, I was a married woman with limited access to her voice.

I didn't have much of a role model when it came to marriage, but I knew that my situation was far from ideal. It was not my expectation. After all the chasing he did to get me, I could not understand why he didn't value what I brought to the relationship. It made no sense that he wanted me so badly at first, but then he started being utterly disrespectful to me.

When it came to his mother, I was second-best on the back burner. Mister knew who I was when he got with me. He knew that I was starting over and trying to build myself from scraps basically. I didn't have the means to do anything financially. So, I was stuck, and he wasn't the type of husband to invest in his wife. Because his income was grand and his mother was able to supply the job stability, together they were able to get what they wanted. If he wanted anything that required a credit check and a stable job, they worked as a team to get it. I wasn't even a factor when it came to any decision making. Multiple vehicles throughout the whole marriage with no input from the wife. Some men would rather the woman have all the jewels and bling to make them look good, but not in my case. It was never about me. Mister was all for self when it came to a lot of things. He would never invest in me the way a husband should. I invested all of what I had in him; I looked forward to investing even more in him when my situation improved.

Now the Bible says in Genesis 2:24, that **'a man leaves his father and mother and is united to his wife, and they become one flesh.'**

That didn't happen with Mister and me. His mother's role and mine were completely wrong. The lines were blurred out or something. I had no clue that I needed to lay these ground rules at the beginning of my relationship with him. That was a first for me. It was a heartbreaking feeling that I couldn't even speak on. I desired to let them know how I felt and that I wanted it to stop. She knew the Bible inside and out, so she knew that she no longer held the number one position in her son's life. In fact, she taught me a thing or two about walking with the Lord. She just wasn't applying it to our marriage. I believe that it wasn't done intentionally to hurt me; it was more out of habit because they were used to depending on one another.

So, maybe shame on me for not figuring everything out in the early moments. I should have taken more time to check his inventory instead of rushing into something because of missing something from someone else. I definitely should have spoken up before the marriage. Truthfully, I have nothing against her because I know she loved me as if I really were her daughter. I felt her love very deeply. There was nothing that she wouldn't do for me and my daughter. She expressed that time and time again. Her exact words have always been, "If anything ever happens between you and my son, you will always be my daughter-in-law and Justice will always be my granddaughter." In my naivety, I accepted those words as a positive message, not knowing that it would truly be the outcome of our marriage. What I know is there is power in words. (Proverbs 12:18)

♡

The longer I stayed with him the more I felt that the marriage wasn't right. That marriage had to end. I finally made a choice for myself. For us. I decided to leave my marital home. I finally told myself that I will not be the woman that stays with a man just because we have kids together. I wanted more. I was tired of him coming and going as he pleased. He was no longer respecting anything concerning his vows to me. The thought of my children growing older and believing that living the way we were was acceptable made me cringe. I couldn't let that happen.

What if his behavior gets worse?

I felt like my walls were closing in and I had to make a decision. So, I did.

I premeditated and was able to get my own apartment for me and the kids. I felt like a part of me was dying inside the whole time that I was trying to find a place and help to move without him knowing. Thankfully, I was able to pull it off. I wasn't honest with him because I wanted to hurt him. I wanted him to hurt like I had been hurting. I wanted to see him show some kind of emotion. I wasn't honest with him about moving because I didn't want him to try to talk me out of a life-changing choice I made. I put my security deposit down and called my Uncle Kevin and Uncle Muffy for help. They were willing to help me out with one stipulation: they didn't want to be in the middle of us going back and forth with each other. They wanted us to figure it out and not start the vicious cycle of breaking up to make up. Uncle Kevin was adamant about that. Of course, I was his niece before anything, but Uncle Kev was cool with Mister too. He loved us both and wanted the best for us.

The morning of the move was very painful. I almost decided not to do it. I had to wake my husband up from his sleep to tell him that I was leaving him. The look on his face and the brokenness that his heart may have been feeling made me queasy to my stomach. I just wanted to hug my husband and believe all his words we had in our kitchen before I left. We both were very emotional about what was about to take place. We shed a few tears, hugs and kisses as he began to tell me he knew that he wasn't all that he could be to me and that I deserved better from him. He promised me that he would get himself together. Uncle Kev told him, "Don't worry, Champ, you will get her back after you get yourself together."

His words gave us both some much needed hope.

Chapter Seven

As the kids and I were settling in and enjoying our new home, I realized that my healing would take place between those walls. I didn't tell Mister where my place was right away. I wanted time to get settled in first. However, once he knew he was coming over to make sure we were ok and that we were able to function properly in our new setting. We still planned family time and sleepovers. It's like we didn't miss a beat with each other.

Some kind of separation, right? Of course, he was still doing what he wanted to do especially since he had extra room to do so.

The "separation" was short-lived. I had my apartment for about 8 months. You can't even call that a real separation. He didn't want his wife to get too far away. The kids and I would go stay at his place and he would either stay at mine or come over before I had to leave out for work so he could take care of the kids. It was almost like we were dating each other again. I was really missing my husband. We were flirting with each other and it felt good. The next moment I looked up and I was moving my things back into our home. The kids didn't seem bothered by any of the changes. They were so young, and they were used to seeing us all together. That brief separation didn't allow any time for us to discuss why we were even separated in the first place. It may have been a conversation here or there, but we were more concerned with missing each other or getting back to our norm.

The kids and I moved back home. Our family was being restored and we were all elated to get back to our regularly scheduled program. I missed him so much. I missed all the things that come along with a two-parent home--the live-in help and our kids not having to go to different houses. We were back on track and my husband was ready to be the husband that God created him to be.

We were all doing wonderfully until the old behavior began to surface. *Here we go again.* Before I knew it, Mister was getting smart, being rude, and acting all macho like I didn't matter again. I needed to do something differently. I wanted to figure out a plan to save my marriage for the last time. I tried everything under the sun. Honey, I had my thinking cap on. Time had passed and I didn't know what else to do.

We had not been intimate, and he was running around outside the house doing who knows what. One time comes to mind when I so desperately wanted to spend time with him. My yearning for him to hold me went unfulfilled. He said that he was on his way to meet his boy. I pleaded with him to stay at home so we could spend some quality time together. I said so much to him that evening and before I knew it, I was offering to give him oral sex to stay.

He declined my gesture.

He told me 'no' and left out the door like I asked him if he wanted a sandwich. My thoughts were trying to add up how he had just declined my services to go hang out with his friend.

I'm done.

That's when I knew that he had been gone emotionally. No man in their right mind says 'no' to oral sex! Heck, even strangers want that from each other.

Eventually, I began to do the same thing as him. I was just going through the motions. I was checking out but still present. Faithfully, I still handled all my mommy and home duties, as well as be there for my husband when he wanted me to. Yet, he was still coming and going as he pleased. He said as few words as possible and only uttered when he had no other choice but to talk to me. That was fine with me after a while. I would rather not engage with a person that looked at me like I stank or talked to me with so much attitude. You would have never thought that we said, 'I do.' Once I began to adapt to the terrible changes again, it started to look like we were having an upside start to our life. He was beginning to come around. He was washing clothes, cooking, and doing other things around the house.

Ok, Mister, I see you!

♡

Once again, the changes didn't last long.

I had to be at work at 7am one day in February. It was bright and early because I worked about an hour away at a high school. I was setting up at work when I began to get calls and texts from a few people that I socialized with on our street. Finally, my supervisor was off my back and I was able to look at the messages and calls. It was kinda confusing. I was wondering what they were talking about. Then it finally hit me, and I felt like I was about to lose my mind. I read some of the messages:

"How are you going to move without you telling me?"
"What's up with this moving truck and your husband out here?"

   I know this guy ain't moving out while I'm at work.

The thought of the whole ordeal was shocking to me. The previous few days would have never made me think that is where his state of mind was.

I tried to call him but no answer. Called again. No answer.

Next, I called my mom and she confirmed the scene from my text messages when she arrived at my house. When I arrived at my home, I was in shock because not only was there a moving truck, but he had the police there too! My chest felt like I had cinder blocks on it. The heaviness was not due to the police presence, but reality hit me hard. Initially, I was confused as to why the police were there. He wanted to make sure my frail %#@ wouldn't do anything to him or stop his process. Go figure. His so-called friend was there to help him leave his wife.

This dude.

I was deeply hurt but I still tried to have a conversation with my husband. It was useless; he was so high on his horse. He had it going on. He had it going on for himself, not his family. What was his was his and what was mine was mine. There was no getting through to him.

This is marriage?!

Not what I ever expected or learned in my years of my earlier relationships. David would always make sure I had more than what I needed or ever dreamed of. I knew better.

This isn't it honey!

So, I welcomed the change that was happening. I was about to go through all those grieving steps again. Only that time I had to face the changes differently.

Again, I couldn't go to certain areas because of another crippling loss. First, the reminded thoughts of David being taken from me and then my husband walking out. Another road less traveled because I didn't want to be reminded of the places we went together. You couldn't get me to go to Monroeville. If I had to go to Penn Hills, it was a chance I would go into a whole panic attack. It was awful because that's where I handled business and did my grocery shopping. Most of my family lived there so I would instantly get sad because I wanted so desperately to not feel that way. Anger would manifest if my mom or anyone forgot that I was carrying that crippling pain around with me.

It was like having PTSD times two. I prayed to God every day:

> *Please don't let me see anyone I know. Please don't let me run into him with this broad or one of these multiple broads that I was told he was with.*

I was never the type to go looking for any information, but it always came to me. I had to tell my family and close friends that I wasn't interested in hearing anything else about Mister. Things would come to me and before I could get a chance to reject the information.

"I saw your husband with this one or that one."
"Some big booty girl with hair down her back and makeup."

It baffled me that he was into women who were the total opposite of me because he expressed contrasting expectations for me. Mister asked me to be a plain Jane. Just wear a natural wrap and no makeup ever. It was easy to live with his request because that has always been me. Pure beauty is what a friend of mine calls it.

> *In my mind and heart, he's gone. Just like David. Another victim of getting caught up in the street life.*

Yes, I was grieving the loss of another relationship, except it was due to women coming between us. One of the most hurtful things came as a phone call from my big cousin. One evening, I was on my way home from work and she called me as she often did. She is one of my favorite people. I was working at Verizon, way out in Cranberry, so the ride home was a long ride and I spent it chatting with her. As we talked, I could hear something wrong in her voice. What she was about to tell me could have been anything. With a huge family like ours, who knows the words that were about to leave her tongue. Once they did, I was in tears. I'm sure it wasn't easy for her to share, but I needed to know. My wonderful husband had exchanged phone numbers with her friend, and they were planning to get together soon.

> *Okay, playa! You want to meet and plan greetings with someone in the GetGo parking lot 81 days after you said 'I do' in St. Thomas?*

Not only had he planned to meet up with her, but he ran our whole situation down to the chick. The wedding, location, attendees, type of job he had, my family name, and where my family was from. The whole nine. So, when the female told my cousin about the prize package that she just met and how she was looking forward to hooking up with him, red flags instantly went up. As my cousin quietly listened to her friend ramble on about her new guy, she figured out very easily who she was talking about. Tink and Mister! There was no way that I could keep it all in.

When I made it home, I calmly confronted him even though I didn't really have the strength to deal with any of it. I shared what I knew and how I felt without revealing my source. But again, I let it go. He asked for forgiveness and I wanted to give him another chance. *People make mistakes, right?!* Live and learn is what I was hopeful for.

But that time he made a choice to leave.

There was no way that I should have received his ring. I was already carrying so much pain in my heart when he came into my life. Don't get me wrong, I loved my husband very much and still love him. I would have given my all to save our marriage. However, we both came with lots of baggage. In retrospect, I can say that neither one of us was ready to take that step to be accountable for the other. I was ready for the kind of husband that I needed for where life had me at the moment and he needed the kind of woman that wanted the same things he desired.

I was still trying to cope with losing David and having this ugly disease called Post Traumatic Stress Disorder. Yes, I have PTSD. I had no idea that I had this for a long time. I went to many doctors and was finally told that there is a name for what I was experiencing. This is a profoundly serious condition. I'm not proud of it but I was the chosen one, so I had to roll with it.

My husband never asked me about what happened to me or even asked me to tell him the story from start to finish. So many have asked me what happened out of love for me. It almost felt like they wanted to connect with me so they could experience it with me. The feedback from those different people was amazing. Some would tell me their feelings when they saw me on the news. It made me cry knowing that I was loved and cared about. Maybe he didn't want to be emotionally connected or maybe he was busy with what he had going on within himself. However, I felt that when we came into a relationship, the best thing that we could have done was spend time forming a close bond with one another. He was my person and we should have gotten to know each other. I have always been a transparent person, so if he even once allowed himself to open up to know me more, I know that he would have loved me on a deeper level. As the kids say, there are levels to this. The deeper the levels, the deeper the connection. In my relationship, I couldn't express that I had a sickness. I had to hide it the best I could.

I would have moments when I was incapacitated or couldn't leave out of my house and sometimes the bedroom. I questioned myself if I was able to openly express what I was going through without feeling like damaged goods and the answer was no. Once or twice I tried to share but after the rejection from him, because he didn't care enough or wasn't educated enough about my illness, I had to keep it to myself. That is the last thing to do to a person that has gone through such a traumatic situation. Thank God I made it through that storm.

If I can just reach one person involved with a person that experienced PTSD, my advice would be to please be there for them. Ask someone or even Google what you can do to be there for them. Don't ignore the fact that that person went through something before they got with you. If you care, make it known that you care. If not, leave them be. Someone better will come along to help them. In all fairness, Mister wasn't aware that I had this illness, but there were certainly signs that were ignored where he could have helped his wife. I made continuous trips to see different therapists all the time. Yes, he occasionally asked questions, but I knew that he wasn't really interested in the answers.

After several doctors/therapists and still not knowing what was wrong with me, a doctor finally was able to diagnose me. I tried two doctors in Ohio and maybe four in Pittsburgh. No one ever told me what was wrong. I just kept starting my story over from the beginning and leaving them three to six weeks later to find another therapist. Then, I finally met someone that started to make me want to continue therapy for the timeframe that she suggested. She was able to shed light on what was wrong with me.

I finally had a diagnosis. I finally understood so many things that were going on with me. Why I had sadness on and off again. Why I couldn't go to certain places without panic attacks. Why I had a strong sense that I wasn't going to make it through the day because I couldn't catch my breath. I was so grateful to know what was going on so I could begin my new journey to try to heal as much of me as possible. I knew it wasn't going to be easy, but I was determined to save my life. I started to try out different things. I watched inspirational speeches or church online if I wasn't able to attend. I wrote down my feelings, thoughts, or even events that happened that I wanted to remember. Outside of therapy, I did whatever I could do to aid in my healing. I was on a mission to become healthy, happy, and whole.

♡

During the five years that we were married, I went through so many things with Mister. I remember so much but I've also blocked out a lot of things. Now that we aren't together, I know that he wasn't to stay as my forever. His place in my life was his place. I had to sit down and talk to myself and God about making another big decision.

God should I really do what I'm about to do?

Once upon a time I used to make decisions without consulting God first but once I knew better, I had to take it straight to him. With all my heart, I believe I received the green light to file for divorce, so I did.

I began the divorce process a few months after he left. I wanted to give it some time to settle down so I wouldn't feel rushed about my next move. I needed to make sure that I wasn't jumping the gun. I found my attorney and began to travel down the long road to divorce. It was a long, expensive road! As I began the divorce process, I started to remember things in my marriage that used to hurt me. Some words were said to me to make me feel that I was nothing or that my existence didn't matter. There were so many times that I felt worthless. A few times I decided to leave for a few days to give us some time apart. One time I left, I only went to my grandmother's house, which wasn't far. It was a place where he wouldn't have to guess where I was. When I decided that a few days was enough and I was ready to go sleep in my own bed, I went home to a house with changed locks. So, I had to go back to my grandmother's house. I don't know how long the locks had been changed, but I was locked out of my own home and in a vulnerable state. I had to wait until he was good and ready for him to come and get us. I was convinced that meant that we had to wait until he was done playing in the streets. What other reason would he have locked his wife and kids out? Although I knew that it wasn't right and it wasn't a good feeling, I still wasn't quite ready to move on without him. So, I waited. I waited for him to give me permission to go back into *our* home.

With the man I married being served with divorce papers, I felt sad but happy because there was no going back. I was done done. I had to pay for a courier to serve him because I wanted no parts of handing him the papers. The court appearances were starting, and I was dealing with relived memories of going to court for the trial of the cowards who took David away from me. He wasn't civil at court in any way. Every time we had to attend court he would make it so hard for me. It was like he never loved me. He was shouting things out while we were there that would make me want to just crawl up in a ball and die. The dirty looks and comments that he would say to me and about me were terrible. He would have conversations on his phone with people saying some of the nastiest things about me. I had no one to go to court with me to help keep him from attacking me but I also wanted to deal with it on my own. I tried my best not to involve too many people. I needed to ride that one out alone.

"You won't be nothing without me! I made you; you will be right back living with your grandma!"

I wasn't sure what he meant by that. If he made me, he did a poor job. I was more broken at that point than I had ever been. I didn't have any confidence and my self-respect was limited. I was broken!

After all the months of going through negotiations, I just wanted it to be over. Often, I would put my head down and pray that the Lord wouldn't let him see me cry. On the drives to the courthouse and before I walked into any courtroom or offices that we both had to be in, I would pray some of my hardest prayers ever. If I didn't know how to pray before, I learned how to pray while going through my divorce. I had to high five myself after a prayer sometimes. He played on my emotions so many times and I knew that I needed something bigger than him to protect me.

I gave up on all that I could have fought for during our divorce. I just wanted to stop seeing his face. It felt like I was losing to the devil himself. My divorce decree even took away my liberties of having a man on my terms. Mister had his attorney include language in the decree that prevented me from having a man live in my home for three years. I guess since the decree stated that he was to pay alimony for three years, he added that condition. Out of frustration and desire to just end the whole ordeal, I agreed to the terms. I didn't have a man anyway, so it wasn't a big deal to me. Honestly, that stunt was just another way for Mister to control me. Even after our marriage ended, Mister was still finding ways to control the way I move. It is worth mentioning that to date I have not received one cent of alimony from him.

Part Three

I STILL BELIEVE...

Chapter Eight

I still believe and know God has a special plan for me. About a year or so ago when I was talking to my Nana on the phone, she made me realize that God has always had His hand on my life. She reminded me even more that whatever I went through or was going through that I was going to be ok. My Nana is my godmother, Belinda's, mom. She helped instill some great values in me as well. She would take me to church and pray with me. I was 3 years old when I first started going to church. She told me that I was in church one day with my pretty dress on sitting like a little lady. She looked down at me and asked me what I was doing. Well, my brilliant response was, "I'm rolling me a reefer." Of course, I wasn't actually rolling one; it was some tissue in my hands. There are a few other stories about my smart mouth, but it was all learned from something I saw or heard. Belinda would also encourage me to say some smart stuff that she would crack up at.

When I was still living in York as a young kid, I was supposed to go stay at my paternal grandmother's house with my cousins. Well, to make a long story short, that never happened. I ended up staying at my Nana's that night. The news headlines the next day shared the tragic story that my cousins died in a house fire--a house fire where I was supposed to stay the night before. If my Nana had not requested that I stay with her and her family all weekend, I would have been just a kid that was from York, Pennsylvania with a short life lived. My mom would have lost her only child because I was all she had. Talk about God having His hand on me! Of course, my heart was saddened for my family losing their kids, but the ordeal was yet another eye-opener. I really do have a purpose here. I could have been gone. No Justice or Leon. No meeting all these people that I love. I'm so determined to figure out why my God has me here and the plan He has on my life. Why He chose me.

With that being said, I have never held anything against my uncle, who I will never name in this book, for the way he treated me the night I lost my David. I was a young adult and the way he made me feel could have really done more harm to my mental health if God wasn't with me. I think my mindset was that my family was going to all come together and make sure I was ok in those times of need. Especially him. I felt like I had a baby that needed me to be okay, so my family was going to save me. But that didn't happen. More and more thoughts come to mind and it continues to dampen my spirits when I think back to that phone call. That is one of those moments where I can truly understand why God wants us to depend on Him and not man (Psalm 118:8). I don't even remember praying during the whole kidnapping ride. But I know now that God has always had my back, front, and everything in between. I had my moments at the beginning of my healing stages where I was angry with my uncle, but I never ever expressed it to him. I may have said a few things to close relatives but never directly to him. There is really nothing to say to him about it. I don't need to tell him how I feel. It won't bring my love back. I don't carry a grudge against him. What's the point of that? I still show him respect because that is my grandmother's son and my mom's brother, but I don't ever need to speak to him about it. When I see him, which isn't often, I say 'hey', maybe give a hug, and make sure I tell him that I love him. Because I do. My teaching of the Bible tells me to love those that persecute us and love our neighbors. (Matthew 5:43-48) However, I will never be ok with having one-on-one time with him because that was buried back in 2003.

The Bible has also taught me to exercise wisdom. So, I will love him and use wisdom not to be around him for long periods of time because it's not good for me. I have learned to forgive a man that never asked for forgiveness. That forgiveness is for me. That's my peace. God has given me the strength to endure so much and through all this I have learned just how perfect His strength is when I am weak.

After I was kidnapped my life felt so upside down. I felt like I didn't have any reason to live because I had worked so hard to get what was stolen from me. However, once I got to my healing, I felt like I had so much to live for. I was starting a new family and I was happy again. I was able to smile again. I was so tired of being alone and sad from losing one of the best men that ever came into my life. I was about to start a new relationship with a man that I would quickly discover wasn't spiritually ready to be with a woman like me. But I still believed...

I wanted a real family that had meals together, spent time together, and enjoyed one another. That's all I ever wanted but was stopped in my tracks each time I got close to achieving it. I was looking for what I had with one man with another man that wasn't ready or even able to comprehend what I needed for the life that I desired. It took me so many years to heal from David's passing. I still have so much to work through, but God has shown up so many times over the years. I have been taught that He is a faithful God, so I've learned to expect to see God daily.

David's murderers and my ex-husband took something away from me that I thought was forever. Something that I always wanted more than anything in the world--a family! It was removed from my hands not once, but twice.

As I have now come to realize that I am healed in *some* of those tender places but not all. It takes me back to when Jesus walked and was being persecuted. He said, "Father, forgive them, for they do not know what they are doing." (Luke 23:34) Those men that did all that to me and my family were sick people, just like those men that did that to Jesus. To take apart a family with your hands and words is a selfish act. I will never understand all the reasons why and I'm not going to even try. But I will say, I believe that all this had to happen for me to be able to serve my purpose here on earth.

Whatever God wants me to go through I will. His will be done!

♡

It took me about three years to heal from the broken pieces that my divorce left me with. I was forced to pick up each piece one by one and put my life back together. Today, I'm still finding pieces that I missed that require attention. When I do find those pieces of debris, I pray and I fast and I pray some more. I go into straight survival mode. It took a good friend to tell me that's what I'm doing. Every day, I am trying to survive. I've become a beast at surviving. Don't get me wrong, I have failed at it many times. Trying to survive is no joke but I have learned what helps me.

I began blocking all outside noise. I built up that wall that 45 talks about. Praise and worship were and still are my go-to. I cut out and limited so many things from my life and daily routines such as old school rap (my favorite) and R&B music. I don't watch gossip T.V. shows or entertain negative conversations. I won't go to certain areas that may trigger my bad thoughts. I was taught by my pastors and elders to feed myself and lay hands on myself when I am feeling weak, pain or depleted. God has given us the power to touch and heal just like He gave His Son.

I don't think I will ever be completely healed from losing David but each year that passes is different. I never know how I'm going to feel around his rise to heaven. Whichever way it goes, I make sure that I acknowledge God in all of it because without Him, none of this would be possible. If it wasn't for my husband leaving me--*correction*--if it wasn't for my ex-husband being removed from my life, I would have never known how strong I am. I have thanked Mister for walking away several times because I would have never realized that I can stand on my own two feet.

On Sunday April 30, 2017, I went to church with the kids and I'm so glad we did. Church was truly a blessing! Not only was it the 14th anniversary of David's death, but it was also the first time in many years that Justice wanted to go to the gravesite to visit her dad. I was more than happy to take her but equally concerned with where she was mentally. I worked my way to the altar to pray. That morning, the Holy Spirit led me to pray for Mitch and myself. As I headed to the altar, my apostle stopped me and said that she believed that Denise had a word for me. Darn if she didn't! As I stood crying, she told me that I needed to finish my book. I needed to do God's work. Something about a platform. I'm going to touch people from all over. All I need to focus on is God's work. She kept saying I need to make a decision. It's going to come fast. I need to buy a tape recorder, something. Be aware of distractions. He will be 6'2" and dark skin and come with money. Be aware he's just a distraction. He's not from God. Don't worry about how this book is going to happen; God will send people to help you. God will help you write. He will give you the words.

There I was in full shock! I hadn't expressed to anyone at church that I was writing a book and the woman of God knew all my business. Then she told me that a man that is about 6'2" and chocolate with money was going to be a distraction!

> *I'm a single woman with kids, living check to check and this man is going to come with some deep pockets, and he won't*

be a blessing but a distraction! Ok game face on! You will not be able to get past this wall. The devil is a liar, as Ms. Sharon says.

So, there I was again being shown that God had His hands on me and knew how to get my attention. The funny thing is that at the time I was trying to decide about going back to school. On the morning of church, I was certain that I was going back to school to pursue nursing. But nope! God told me 'no' just that quickly by having Denise speak those words to me. I knew I needed to give my book--*I mean God's book*--my all, so I jumped in every chance I got. I began writing like crazy.

On June 17, 2017, I went to my niece's play at her school downtown. She is an exceptionally talented young lady and I enjoyed the play. There were many positive nuggets in it for all ages to pick up. My mind looks for positive things every day and the play gave me handfuls of positive messages. It mainly was about standing out even if you don't feel like you want to and how it only takes one decision to do the right or wrong thing. Just the previous year, I was so nervous about going to her play because I wasn't in a good place. I had even tried to walk through Market Square, and I ran into a few people I knew. I was so scared. I couldn't get out of there fast enough. I didn't want anyone from my past or present to see or talk to me. I figured out of sight out of mind. I saw someone that used to live in Spring Hill when I did. Then I saw someone that I used to work with at Verizon Wireless. Then I saw a friend of the family. Then I saw my aunt. I was so overwhelmed. I wanted to get out of there by a snap of my fingers. But no, I had to walk through the crowds of the stone streets. Well, that was before. The year I attended my niece's play was different. I was healed in so many areas of my life. To God be the Glory! Honey, let me tell you. I parked my car and walked toward Market Square, not even realizing that the Juneteenth celebration was going on.

Let's get it!

My daughter and I walked towards the music as we heard some good tunes blaring. It was a live band playing my kind of music. One of the last songs I heard was Bruno Mars, "That's What I Like." I was lightweight enjoying myself. Of course, my child was looking at me like, *mom!* But she didn't say a word; she let me have my moment. An older man walked up to me and wanted to dance. Now, if I was back at the bar in Ohio, I would have handed my drink to Steph or Precious so I could do my same ol' two-step. Most of the time I would dance with my purse swinging it like it was part of the dance routine. I really wanted to accept his offer and dance, but I didn't want to end up on someone's IG or FB page. I politely declined and we talked. As we chatted, I found out that I went to school with his son. While we were talking, a lady walked up to me and said that I looked familiar as we tried to figure out where she may have known me from. After some time, it registered to her.

She asked, "Do you know David Smith?"

"Yes, that's my daughter's grandfather," I replied. "We buried his son, who was my daughter's father, 14 years ago."

"That's where I know you from," she said, as her eyes began to fill with tears.

As she opened her mouth to speak on the day she met me, her voice began to crack. Her thoughts took my daughter and me back to the day before we buried her father. She said that when she saw my strength on display for hours at his wake, she was hurting for me and my daughter. I began to cry as I recalled some of the same visuals that she mentioned. I couldn't help but want to comfort her since that's my nature to want to take on others' pain. That time was different though. She was expressing *my* pain to me. That was one of the quickest conversations I've had about David through the years. It was also one that touched me deeply. Before I was able to get her name, she darted away from me and said, "I inspired her." I begin to tear up. I was like a kid wanting more from her, but I didn't want to run after her. I was kind of paralyzed and consumed with many thoughts in the middle of that public place. I thought I was going to have to phone a friend to come help me get through what I thought was going to be a PTSD moment. But nope, I was ok! God placed me smack in the middle of busy Market Square. I was fine and I was able to keep it together. It's funny how I was in that same place just a year before and mentally I couldn't handle it. A year later, I was in the same place but not in the same place, if that makes sense. I was prepared to run away and cry with an outbreak of PTSD that would linger on for who knows how long. However, that time I was able to be inspired and move through it more smoothly.

Lord knows that I wasn't ready to tell my daughter about having PTSD in the middle of that place with all these strangers. I didn't want to scare her. I just wasn't ready to out myself to her about my impacting condition.

I'm unsure of what God's plan was with that day, but I knew His hand was on it. I was originally going to the 7 pm show but I decided on an earlier show. If I would have gone to the earlier show, I would have missed the encounters. I started to see some of the pieces come together such as how people are here to help you get to your purpose. That lady in Market Square was supposed to be there for me. She may have thought she was coming to have a good time, but she did something for me that I will never forget. I wish that I could see her again to thank her. She did so much for me that day.

That day caused me to fall in love with God even more. I love my relationship with Him. It's priceless when you can discover new ways to fall in love all over again. In any personal relationship, I believe that rediscovering newness is needed. My personal relationship with God keeps getting that new breath of fresh air and I don't want to ever let it go.

♡

My PTSD started manifesting before I even knew what to call it. That coupled with depression was an elixir for disaster. I recall crying for long periods because I was reliving the visions of what David and I had experienced. My mind wouldn't let me rest during the night and it wouldn't let me work well during the day. My job started to get in the way, so I had to call off due to not being able to focus. I was cautious because if I got fired, that would have invited more depression in. I later had to get official papers to cover my butt from the possible termination. I also sought out a new therapist which wasn't easy. Mainly because I had to keep retelling my story from the beginning and now, I was adding in a dose of divorce.

During my marriage and after my separation, I would have so many moments that PTSD would creep up on me. Some days it wasn't a creep; it came full-fledged. I painfully remember sometimes not being able to go outside for days because I was terrified to leave the house. Sometimes I wouldn't be able to go off the second floor of our house. Leon was young and didn't need to have real food, so it was easy to not have to go downstairs. I couldn't eat because my PTSD would sometimes take over my appetite. I was even substituting Mountain Dew for food. It made me feel full and gave me a little bit of energy. If it wasn't the PTSD taking my appetite, it was my depression. I was screwed. When I was finally separated and going through my divorce, PTSD was one of the worst things for me to experience.

While I was going through my divorce, I was not showering for days at a time. The thought of being in a closed bathroom and shut off from what was going on within the rest of the house seemed unfathomable. I just couldn't do it. I was single and sleeping alone so that was not hard to pull off. It was just the kids and me. I didn't have any adults living in the house with me to question why I was crying or not bathing. The kids may have asked me why my eyes were red but nothing about not getting cleaned up. None of my family knew about this until one day I was able to find the courage to tell China what I had gone through. It wasn't that I thought people would judge me; I just didn't know how to put my challenges into words.

There was a time when I needed to go to East Liberty to see my divorce lawyer to sign some papers. As I drove towards the area, I started to feel different. My fear slowly crept up on me because the guys that killed David were from the area where I was headed. The feeling began to get more and more intense. As I pulled up, I was able to find a parking spot right in front of the building.

Sigh of relief.

I got out of my car, walked to the door, and rang the bell. I rang the bell again. No buzz for the door to open. I began to break out in what felt like an internal sweat. I didn't feel anything on the outside of my body. It was all inside. I quickly walked back to my car and began to cry uncontrollably. I couldn't stop. As much as I thought that I was getting myself together I wasn't. I picked up my phone to call whomever I thought would answer. Surprisingly, no one answered. I couldn't believe no one was available.

China always answers her phone for me it seems, but she must be busy.

I felt so alone. I had to have called at least four people. I was able to get myself together enough to drive around the corner, which was the back of the building. As soon as I was able to park, I let out screams and cried so loud. I didn't care who heard or saw me at that point.

Lord help me! Show me what it is You want of me at this time.

After more unsuccessful calls to my lawyer, I drove off towards Lincoln. I was going to either go to see Ms. Penny or my Uncle Reece. I thought for sure that one of them would be home, but no one was home!

She's always home when I stop by.

God showed me once again that it was a Him and I moment. He wanted me to depend on Him fully. He wanted me to learn, yet again, to take care of me. Eventually, I was able to get it together.

♡

I never wanted to move back to Pittsburgh. EVER IN LIFE! They say if you want to make God laugh, tell Him your plan. Well, he brought my butt back right back here and took me through all the areas that I thought I would never step foot in again. God dropped me right in the middle of it. Boom! The way God works is He will do and use anything or person to get your attention. God used my ex-husband in a good way. He took me to my most painful area to make me grow. The Bible says, **"For God hath not given us the spirit of fear; but of power, and of love, and of a sound mind." (2 Timothy 1:7)** This verse speaks so deeply to me as well as other verses about being fearful. I was so afraid to come back to Pittsburgh because I just knew that I wouldn't be able to handle the constant memories of the things that I witnessed here. The good memories were no longer able to be felt. Only the bad. I know that God gave me what I wanted. He knew I wanted to feel taken care of and that I wanted a father for my daughter. Well, He answered my request and some. I asked for what I wanted instead of praying for what I needed. I remember when I stopped being afraid and when the thoughts about me dying young left. A sound mind was the best gift that I was given. It was like a weight was lifted off my shoulders. I was visiting a church, Sound the Alarm Ministries. It was the church's anniversary, so they had a guest preacher from Philly. I didn't know what to expect but I felt that I was going to get something by traveling to this church that was about an hour away. I was expecting to meet God there and I couldn't wait. I could have jumped in the church van, but I decided to drive. I wanted to enjoy the drive to and from. I knew I was ready for what was coming from this service. It would be yet another divine appointment.

The preacher delivered one of the best messages I have ever heard. I felt like I was at a big conference in one of the mega churches in Dallas. Next thing I knew, he called me out of my seat.

"You come here."
I hesitated.
"Yes you."

I walked toward him, and he gave me one of the best words I have received thus far. The details were so far-fetched, but I knew that it could only be God. How else would he have known my life hurts? It was one of those moments that if you didn't believe in God, it would have all changed after that encounter. Pastor Brown said so much to me that I can't wait to see it all come to pass. One thing that stood out was that he told me to ask the people who love me for help. I listened to that advice and things started happening for me. I'm glad I did too; I never want to have a prideful heart. A few things have already manifested but the best is yet to come.

A similar experience happened to me when I went to a church for the first time. I now call it my home church. My Apostle had no clue who I was or my story, but she said something to me that left me with tears. Everything that she said to me let me know that I was in the right place. I had no worries that I was in good hands.

Through all this, I've learned to stand on my own and to have my own identity. I'm finally able to not stand behind a man. I have shed the need to feel like I have to say I'm David's fiancé or Mister's wife. I am my own person. As I've said before, I'm so appreciative of my pain. I no longer have to stand behind anyone or use a man to validate who I am. No, I am Lakeenah! If anything, I will stand beside a man that I am one with. I may not be educated with degrees from top universities or community colleges or I may not pronounce every word correctly or spell like I'm a scholar, but I know who I am and the woman I want to become. I'm a woman that has been educated in what love is and what love isn't. I've been educated in heartache, pain, and suffering. Educated on love and abandonment. Educated on how to bury the man that I thought you would spend the rest of my life with. Educated on how to put my heart, body and soul back together from someone tearing me down to the point I thought I couldn't get back up. But I did! That's where my education lies. It didn't cost me 100's of thousands of dollars but it did almost cost me my life.

I know I had to unexpectedly go through the grieving stages twice. Some may question why I didn't see either situation ending the way it did. But I truly didn't. No matter how you look at it whether prepared or unprepared, strong or weak, deserving or undeserving, it still hurts. I still had to go through all the grieving orders.

While grieving over my double loss of love, I had to endure the hard process of losing my uncle. I got a phone call at 2:00 a.m. It was Mom Mom calling, but I could hardly understand the words that she spoke.

"TINK TINK, they shot Kevin! They shot Kevin!"

Those words continue to play over and over in my head till this day.

I didn't know who *they* were, but I needed to know where I should be headed. I hung up with her and I began to pray so hard while crying a silent cry because I had to be a mom first to protect my kids until I knew exactly what was going on. I got dressed so quickly. I woke my daughter to let her know that I had to leave and not to worry. I told her that I would be right back. She trusted my words and went back to her peaceful sleep.

I made it to my destination in the rain in less than 12 minutes from the time I got the call. Mom Mom didn't say anything about him being dead, nor did I think that either. I instantly went back into prayer mode. I prayed all the time so that was nothing out of the ordinary. I prayed so hard the whole ride up until I laid eyes on his wife. I just knew that the only thing my family needed at that moment was prayer and I was able to do that. I never thought that he wasn't alive or that he wasn't going to make it because I knew my Uncle.

> He's a survivor and strong. Whatever went down, he can handle his own. His hands are big, and he can lay a punch, like a Mike Tyson punch out. Hell, his looks alone will knock you out when he's mad. But when he's not, his looks can put you in a daze also. So many of my friends call to say how fine my Uncle Kevin is. I always respond, "And he smells good too." With so much emotion, they quip back, "I KNOW!"

I walked straight to my Aunt and I looked into her eyes as tears were falling down my face and I told her that I love her.

"I know you do, Tink. I love you too."

When I got to the street so many were standing around with support for one another. Then more people began to arrive. You know like a family does in crisis or good times. I was still okay because I had prayed for all of us.

> We shall overcome, right?

121

We weren't allowed to go where the police were. I understood because the police needed to do their job. We were standing near a crime scene. They needed to question any witnesses, and of course my Uncle.

But why isn't his wife down there with him at least?

Another family member pulled up and that's when I found out that what I had been praying for wasn't going to actually happen. The family member blurts out the words to my aunt, "Is Kevin dead, Lisa?" He showed no compassion and his question lacked any care. I looked around as if I needed to see the reactions of other people. They were sad but nothing changed with that question being asked. Then, I started doing the math.

There's no ambulance.
His wife isn't down there with him.
We are all standing so far down the street.

Very calmly, I walked to my loving aunt and asked what he was talking about. She confirmed the tragic news that I didn't want to hear.

"It's true, Tink."

At that point, it was more of a downpour of my tears. I wanted to lose my mind! I just didn't know what my body was supposed to do at that moment.

Lord, are You telling me that I have been up here crying and praying and I am the only one that didn't know he was gone? That his soul has already left his body? That I will not be able to say goodbye or see you later?

I kept it together as much as possible because I knew she needed the support more than ever. Lord knows, I again felt like life was leaving out of my body.

He was more like a dad to me and so many others. He wanted the best for me, and I felt it in my heart. He always went above and beyond. My family and close friends are still feeling the effects of his absence. My uncle said something to me and that I will never forget. We weren't having a conversation about anything in particular, but as we sat on my Mom Mom's back porch, he said to me, "Tink, don't go back." He said those words to me just a few weeks before he passed away. When he spoke, I took it in. Once I realized what he was talking about I proudly said that I would not go back! I promised to honor his request. I knew the love my uncle had for me and I know he saw something special in me. I'm glad I see it in myself now. One thing I truly wish is that my uncle could see me in my happy place. I would love for him to see that I am ok and that I am on my way to where I'm supposed to be in life.

I recall trying to comfort his wife, my aunt. I told her that I didn't know what she was going through, and she quickly replied, "You do know, Tink. You have been here before." At that moment, I realized that my pain could really be used to help someone going through a similar situation.

♡

As I sit here, the thought came to me that the only person that may have been able to find out what really happened to David or how this happened is no longer here. I never thought to have a conversation with him. He may have already known who went where. I will never know. If he did know, he protected me from the truth. For whatever reason. Sometimes it's better not to know, so they say. My prayer is to sit down one day with the creeps who took David away and ask why. I don't know when or if I will ever allow myself to truly grieve the passing of my family. Not that I don't want to, but I feel that if I don't grieve, I can pretend like they are still with me. It's easier for me to go on with life and laugh and reminisce as if they are still here. I'm not sure if that is healthy but it feels good.

Chapter Nine

Time is moving fast and I'm trying my best in my new life to keep my head up and to keep finding happiness. I'm doing well now with the hand I have been dealt. I must say it is quite amazing to see how far I've come. A friend of mine once told me that I was a Debbie downer. She said that I was always so sad, even in my conversation. When she told me that I realized that I was carrying around a lot of sadness. I noticed that I talked more negatively than positively. I needed to change even more. I have been working hard to stay out of that space. I no longer want to take up residency in Sadville. I want to be that happy person I once was. That person that is outgoing and fun. That person that would say the craziest stuff to people and laugh plenty. I don't want to be scared to be around people or scared that people will judge me because of what I have been through. I was able to see what my friend meant for myself. I had to get rid of Debbie for the last time. I don't want to be bothered with Debbies anymore. The greatest love of all is self-love. Self-love is the most precious love of all. When you learn to love yourself, you can love people in the way they should be loved. The old saying is, treat people how you want to be treated. The way I want to be treated at all times is with love. Because now, I love myself more than

I have ever loved myself. I will work hard for the rest of my days to keep loving me.

When you operate in the ways that you want, you invite what you want. It's the law of attraction, right? Being loving or positive will have that kind of attraction coming to you. When I began to take inventory of myself, I saw that I am really a nice, genuine person. I never change no matter who I am interacting with. I didn't understand how I was able to be so loving to so many, even strangers. But that's the way God designed me. I thought something was wrong with me until now! Now, I embrace myself. It's ok to love and show love. That's more of what the world needs.

So many have told me that I need to stop being so nice. I tried it (*in Tamar's voice*) and it made me feel terrible. However, what I did learn from all the voices is that you cannot stop being who you are supposed to be. I shouldn't have to stop being nice, loving, caring just because other people in the world don't want to be. What I should have been told to do is stop allowing people in my circle that aren't deserving of who I am or of my love. I love to be me. It's a beautiful feeling. That's what I want to be remembered as. **The woman that loves to love**. I want people to see my glow before you see my face.

I used to wait for permission to move on or be happy and to live again. Please don't mimic that behavior. Stop waiting for permission to move on with your life even when your life isn't ok. Keep at it. Keep adding to it. Keep it moving. People still want to see you be ok. Someone is always watching or secretly rooting and praying for your natural glow to come back to your face.

Through the years since I've become saved, I have encountered so many people who don't believe in God or Jesus or either. Never have I judged or tried to make people change their minds about our Savior. To each his own. I am a believer and I know believing saved my life. His Word and Him loving me with his guaranteed promises are what brought me out of depression and everything else that comes with a broken heart or grieving. So many put their all into people. My thought is people let us down daily so why not at least try to put your faith in someone that says He will guarantee these wonderful things. Who will never leave you. Who will keep you close through the difficult times. I've heard things like it's man-made and why Jesus or this happened to other people in the Bible days, why is He the Messiah, etc. Well, this happened to me and when I was on what felt like my death bed, my mustard seed of faith is the only thing that brought life back to my soul. I felt like I was resurrected from the dead. Once I started to have life back in me, I knew that I never wanted to turn away from that kind of love. I knew that I wanted to know more and more and more. I am greedy for this love that I get by believing and applying it daily. I always want more. First thing in the morning and last thing at night, I speak to God to tell Him thank you and a few other things. I am forever grateful and will continue to be.

God has done some amazing things within me and I want him to continue to bless me according to who He created me to be. So, if I must endure a few people that have been mean and nasty to me just because they aren't able to see my true self then that's what I will do. That's on them; it's not my problem. Take that up with God. God places us in people's lives for a reason. Maybe my reason to be in the lives of those people is to show kindness or love, maybe even strength. Maybe it's to give them something that they never had. Perhaps it's to show them that it's ok to love openly or wholeheartedly. So be it. I'm the woman for the job!

As I began to write this book, I desperately wanted to stop crying but I couldn't. I couldn't wait another day for God to dry my eyes forever of all these painful tears. I wanted Him to replace them with tears of joy and tears of undying happiness. I wanted it NOW! But he didn't move immediately to remove the pain. He kept his hands on me daily. I see that now. He kept renewing my strength (Isaiah 40:31) daily like he said he would. He kept allowing me to be who He made me to be. He kept me in my mess for days, weeks, and months that lead to years. He continued to purge my mind, body, and soul. I kept telling myself what others were making me feel--*those tears are a sign of weakness and you can't let them see you cry.* I slowly have been trying to renew my mind during my time of healing. Tears aren't a sign of weakness. I was getting things out of me. I needed to be purged for what is coming. I know there is something good coming. (Isaiah 61:7 double for states I will receive double for my trouble) I have shared some private parts of my life with whoever is willing to read it. I pray that whenever you read my words that you fall in love with me, who I was, who I really am, and who you see me becoming--The Gates of Beautiful. I pray that if you don't love yourself that you will be able to start from this point on loving you some you.

God has shown me that if you want to rebuild, you must tear it down first and then start rebuilding from the ground up piece by piece. Sometimes you have to just let it hurt and appreciate your pain. Some of the roads that I once thought I could never travel again, I can now travel without always relating it to the kidnapping of my family or a memory with Mister. Only God can do something like this. It brings tears to my eyes often how much God loves me so deeply. He LOVES ME! HE LOVES ME! HE LOVES ME!

I was never needy for love nor did I have daddy issues. I don't recall ever feeling like I was missing anything from my biological dad not being in my life. The love was there any time I wanted it. So, for me to choose not to jump into a relationship as soon as Mister left was easy. Being with a person of the opposite sex can be magical and I absolutely love being with a man and being able to express all of me. Catering to my guy as that famous female group expresses. I miss it a lot, but God and I are in control of my life now and I choose to have this me time. I need to take this time out to get to know me and what I am willing to accept in my life. I now have a 16-year-old daughter and a 10-year-old son who are watching and learning from everything I'm doing. I'm their primary example. The only thing they see now is a Mom who is making it happen. I work overtime as much as I can and sometimes a second job. So, my example to them is far more important than settling for some help paying my bills or just to have someone to take me to a comedy show. People that we are around daily are doing this. To each their own. I don't want to settle for that. The devil is a lie and I refuse to allow someone to block my blessings because it's cheaper to keep me or because I'm sick and tired of paying that high cable bill.

With going through all this, I still believe in true love. I really do. With society today, people don't believe in it. It shows that everyone cheats and that it's ok. Nope, I will wait for my heart's desire. (**May he give you the desires of your heart and all your plans succeed. Psalm 20:4**) or (**Delight yourself in the Lord and he will give you the desires of your heart Psalm 37:4**). This is what keeps me grounded. I can wait and I will have what I desire.

I wanted to write this book back in 2003-2004 when I was doing what I thought was healing. I see now that it wasn't my time to write a book. I had so much more work to do. So much more living and learning to do. So much more to experience. I had to wait for the Lord. 1 Corinthians 1:7 says, "so that you are lacking nothing, wait for the revealing of our Lord." That's what I did, and this is what has been produced. My story needed more time to develop. As Mr. Gary would say, "it's not your time, Tink." But now it is my time.

I am incredibly happy with the new and improved me. I have learned how to date myself with a few rules. I will not go to the movies on a Friday or Saturday night alone or on the opening night of a movie. Now that's just asking for too many eyes to be focused on me. Instead, I opt for a Wednesday or Thursday. I have learned how to comfort myself when no one was there or even when I wasn't ready to share what I was going through. When I began to change my thoughts and my actions, everything else began to align. People began to tell me that they could see a glow about me that wasn't a pregnancy glow. I didn't even know that was possible. They saw something different on me. It was God's grace shining through. They saw that I was better, and I didn't look like what I had been through.

I never want to invite sadness in my heart again. I appreciate all the pain and sorrows and now I'm ready to move forward. My genuine smile is back on my face. I laugh and joke so much now. I give encouraging words. I share my wisdom with people. I share my kind spirit with the ones that have come after me with the pain of losing a person due to gun violence or the loss of a relationship. God has chosen me to go before these women or men that may need an ear to listen or a hand to hold as they go through the low and dark times.

I once had a supervisor tell me that I have an infectious personality. A few months after that I asked one of the higher-ups if he could write me a letter of recommendation. He did and it was short and sweet, but those same words were in there--infectious personality. I could not believe that people really enjoyed being around me. It also changed my way of thinking. I don't have to force anything. People want to be around me because they want to. I don't have to beg for anyone's love or attention. The people that are coming into my life are here for a reason as I am in their life for a reason. Those two men helped me see a better me while I was at work. Those two words they spoke meant so much to me. They said it when I needed it the most. God allowed them to share kind words with me because I was able to show them something as well. I couldn't be more grateful for them.

God continuously uses people to keep me motivated so I don't give up. Two times that stick out to me are when he used my kids. On June 6, 2017, I was fixing their plates for dinner and Justice spoke life to me. "Mom, you are a noble woman. You look like a noble woman." She messed me up with that one. She's one that doesn't speak much, but for her to say those words truly touched me. Leon kept asking what her words meant. "Tell me," he begged but I couldn't put it into words. So, I finished making plates and then Googled it. I wanted to give him an answer and better understand myself where she was coming from and DAMN! Her words were powerful beyond measure! God used her to let me know that I would be ok, that I would have all that my heart desires, and that I'm on the right track. I didn't think I was that Proverbs 31 woman yet, but clearly, I am even though I don't have my husband. My baby girl saw that in me! So, my message to you is to keep trusting and believing.

Another time was when my son and I were in Home Depot. He and I have had countless conversations on so many topics. They are mostly about our future and all the vehicles that we are going to have. That conversation was about pickup trucks and U-Hauls. I gave him examples of why we would use a pickup truck versus a U-Haul. I told him that even though pickup trucks are good for small, quick hauls, sometimes you need a U-Haul so you can make one trip instead of multiple trips with a pickup. I then explained when his dad moved out, he got a big moving truck so he could make one trip to get his stuff. My son said to me, "Mom, we can finally have this talk now." Keep in mind we were in the Home Depot parking lot as we made our second trip that day to get paint for the porch steps. What he meant was that we could talk without one of us getting upset about how things were going or how things turned out between our family.

We went home and started painting the steps, eating and then relaxing because the sun was beaming. My thoughts drifted back to the Home Depot parking lot. Leon was right. It felt damn good to be in a good place, knowing we weren't sad anymore. As I told Leon, "I'm fine. Your Dad did me a favor." I explained to him that when he and his sister meet someone, I pray that they accept them for who they are. "If you can't do something the way they expect, it's ok. As long as they accept you for you. If your feet stink sometimes, it's ok. If you are shy it's ok. Don't ever be with someone that does not love all of you."

Through this journey with my faith being number one in this continued healing that I seek, I have begun to see a lot of things come to pass. Some of my prayers are starting to be answered. I wish I would have kept a prayer journal as I had planned to. But I have prayed for many days and nights for me to be able to see a change in certain areas in my life. I prayed for God to allow me to see Him in major parts of my life. I look for God every day and I can admit that I do get to see His work daily. As the verse goes, **"Seek first the kingdom of God and his righteousness and all these things will be added unto you." (Matthew 6:33)** This verse comes to mind when I think of me seeing God's work during my days. One time I stopped at a store before work, but I didn't want to get out because I wanted to keep listening to a gospel song. It had a great message. Eventually, I got out of the car and went into the store. As I got my coffee, a man walked in and he was loudly playing an even better song that caught my attention. I felt like that was nothing but God chasing me down because He knew that I wanted to continue to hear His word. Then another man walked in with his Jaheem music playing on his boombox shortly after. I liked that song also, but I was able to stay focused on the gospel. Oh, that man playing the gospel also purchased my coffee. Soon to follow was complimentary parking. No, I didn't bat my eyes either! I never learned that trick. It was God chasing me down to let me know that He has me right where He wants me.

My most proud prayer is that I am now able to have somewhat of a relationship with Mister. I didn't think this was anywhere near possible, even with the praying. I know that I was praying and taking him to the altar every chance I got, but I didn't put much belief behind it. I have been taught that you need to believe in what you are praying for. I dropped the ball on that one, but God still decided to show up. Mister and I can laugh together. We are now able to have conversations without getting angry about what we went through when we were together or going through our messy court hearings. Mister and I have had some heart to hearts, and it has been rewarding for both of us and our son. We have been able to share more moments together with our son just because. We have even been able to lean on one another for strength. The co-parenting is working out much better and I no longer feel like I am losing my son due to thinking that his dad is trying to brainwash him or turn him against me because he can do more for him financially. My worst thought was that my son felt that he had to pick and choose who he wanted to be with. I am sure this is all the familiar territory of anyone going through a family split. We are learning to trust one another again. We can finally be in each other's company without me feeling like I want to cut him because I flashed back or him being uncomfortable and asking me about things he really doesn't want to know. We came up with a safe word that protects us from going too far. Because we were husband and wife, we shared something and experienced hurt that will never be resolved but we can grow from it.

With all that said, we are good!

Meeting all the people in Ohio and now being able to call one another family is priceless. It was time with these guys that helped me grieve the man that I loved so very much. They allowed me to come into their lives and loved every part of my brokenness.

I still miss and think about David so much. Just seeing our baby girl grow up makes me wish he were here with us. He would be so proud of the young lady that she is becoming. It's so crazy how David is still being the consistent man in our lives. He's still providing for his family here on earth from the heavenly place where he rests his head. David was a great provider and he is still able to set blessings up for us. I know that he still has a hand in our lives down here. He was that kind of guy that took care of his family. There are so many people living and will do nothing for their kids, both men and women. This man truly left a lasting impression on so many people when it came to his heart and loving spirit.

When I first started writing my book there were parts that I wanted to leave out simply because I didn't want to feed the enemy or shine the light on that part of my life that held me captive or that I wasn't proud of. Then I realized that, again, this is my story through my eyes. This is my healing and truth. It's something that I needed to heal from. My kids, my family, and my book have given me a purpose to live. As Mitch said, "If I'm going to tell my story, I need to tell it all." Here it is. *My* story.

Love will happen again one day. I have faith that my Father up above is preparing my future husband for me as I write these words. In fact, He has been preparing him for me even before I was preparing my heart for him. Let the church say amen!

Amen!

Love will continue to be my language. My next chapter is *Happily Ever After*!

Signed with Love,
Lakeenah Le'Shae

Songs of Healing

These songs helped me to work through my healing. May you find peace, comfort and healing in their melodies and lyrics as well.

Hillary Scott- Thy Will
7eventh Time Down- God is On the Move
For King & Country- It's Not Over Yet
MercyMe- Dear Younger Me & Greater
Zach Williams- Chain Breaker
Judy Jacobs- I Feel a Change 4:34
Marvin Winans- Just Don't Want to know
Eddie James- House of Prayer
Jonathan Nelson- God is Blessing & My Name is Victory
Jonathan Butler- Falling In Love With Jesus
Yolanda Adams- I'm Going To Be Ready
Israel Houghton- Moving Forward
Deon Kipping- What's Coming is Better
Smokie Norful- I Need You Now
Tamela Mann- This Place
Koryn Hawthrone- Unstoppable/Won't He Do It

Made in the USA
Monee, IL
07 April 2023